MANEUVERING ROSÉ WINE WITH STYLE

CHARLES SPRINGFIELD

MANEUVERING ROSÉ WINE WITH STYLE

Published in the United States by way of
The Editorial Stylings,
an editorial division of
The Life Stylings of Charles Springfield,
New York, NY
www.charlesspringfield.com

ISBN (paperback): 978-0-578-72092-0
ASIN (Kindle e-book): B08BJG2S3D

PRINTED IN THE UNITED STATES OF
AMERICA

Second Edition June 2020
10 9 8 7 6 5 4 3 2

the dedication

To all the so-called odd balls, underdogs, outcasts, weirdos and
undesirables who have found a way to tap into their light and force
the world to see your brilliance, beauty and brawn.
This is to us and this is for rosé.

the table of contents

: the declaration

I was in awe the moment I saw rosé.

It was simply beautiful.

The colors. Oh My God! I was not expecting such a wide spectrum of hues. There were shades of pinks ranging from pale rose gold to red plum skin, all so striking and alluring and diverse.

Then I was handed glass after glass. They smelled a-maz-ing.

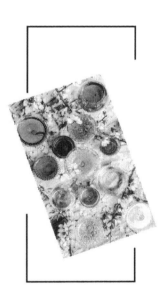

There was a mysterious mélange of fruit, herbs and spice notes: Strawberry. Sea salt. Watermelon. Pink grapefruit. Dried lavender. Ginger. Rhubarb. Jalapeno. Raspberry. Peach. Maraschino cherry.

Then I sipped on them – one by one. They were – wow – so tasty.

While some of the aromas previously listed blew off into the breeze, others were carried through onto the palate in the form of perplexing flavors that were combinations of juicy, tart, earthy and spicy.

It was all so unexpected.

It seems that nestled neatly right between the two larger wine categories, rosé exists. It is not quite a red wine and it most certainly is not a white wine.

It's Rosé. It is a unique category of wines from around the world that are utterly fun and easy to drink.

I didn't know how to articulate those characteristics when I was first introduced to rosé wine. All I knew back then was that I enjoyed everything about it.

That was long before I even knew it was considered wrong.

Yes, wrong to like rosé wines.

Hmm, what? And then why? And lastly, according to whom?

Apparently, that stance was according to a whole slew of wine-loving folks from wine-loving places from France to California.

And it was a belief that lasted multiple decades.

That was confusing to me. I always thought that wine, in the general sense, was one of the more sophisticated adult beverages you could consume.

Although in hindsight, I can remember noticing a fair share of side-eyes, scrunched up faces and clutched pearls over the years in reference to my fascination with rosé.

As it turns out, for most of the 20th century, the elite wine community deemed rosé wine as an unsophisticated, non-wine for wine novices or plebeians – aka – commoners.

Well, damn! Okay.

But what did I know about wine back then? I was just a college kid in the 1990s – who may or may not have been of legal drinking age – trying to explore the world and figure things out.

I've enjoyed wine, all my life, starting at a very young age. But my family and I weren't cellaring and sipping on the 1973 Stag's Leap

Wine Cellars Cabernet Sauvignon from the 1976 Judgement of Paris.

Not by any means. We were casually consuming Moscato d'Asti, Boones Farm and Riunite on ice and thought, at the time, that was rather nice.

When I really think about it now, I can remember a gradual personal wine divide with rosé that started to occur once I graduated college and moved into my professional work settings.

I started my career out as a daily newspaper reporter in New Orleans at the *Times-Picayune* a few weeks after graduation. When taking part in luncheons, attending company holiday parties and going to networking meetings, much of the focus on wine started to revolve around whether you wanted "the red or the white" option. That typically meant either a Cabernet Sauvignon or a Chardonnay.

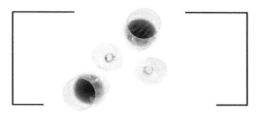

While attending graduate school, I worked at the *Clarion-Ledger* newspaper in Jackson, Mississippi, as an assistant entertainment editor and feature writer. The same options – red or white wine – were mostly presented to me as I attended operas, gallery openings, photography exhibits and poetry showcases.

Then I moved over to the public relations profession after obtaining my master's degree. Client entertaining was very much part of the job in the early 2000s, working for full-service advertising agencies with national and international accounts.

During those times, the wine selections coincided with copious amounts of surf and turf and multi-course dinners while "wining and dining" clients. While the red and white wine selections were a lot more varied during this time, they did not include rosé.

There seemed to be this continuous need for me to concede to the wine desires and tastes of higher ups in the company. They naturally had more elevated drinking experiences than I had at the time, so I chalked it up as part of the corporate grooming process.

I was still figuring out my palate. I was exploring new things to decide what was best suited for me and my personal tastes.

There was no question about what I liked. I knew that. However, there seemed to be a gap forming between what I liked to drink and what was deemed appropriate by others to drink.

In a way, I fell victim to the perfect pairing of propaganda and peer pressure: Judgement. Shame. Insecurity.

Rosé wine would continue to grace my palate from time-to-time over several years. Those times, unfortunately, became less and less frequent.

Then I moved to New York City. Then I started working in the wine business. Then I got reintroduced to rosé.

The popularity of rosé was palpable. It was being consumed everywhere that summer in 2010: the park, the beach, on cruises around Manhattan, on rooftop bars and in the Hamptons.

Rosé was on happy hour lists. Rosé bottles lined multiple store shelves. Rosé was making *New York Times* headlines.

Here we are now, 10 years later, in 2020. Nowadays, everything is coming up rosé.

It's a global movement. It's a vibe. It's a viral hashtag – or several.

From the early spring to the late summer months, one can barely get through the week without someone enthusiastically utilizing the popular hashtags #roséallday, #yesswayrosé and #drinkpink. Then there is even #brosé (bros who drink rosé). Hey, I make it up or co-sign that one.

Rosé has become a regular part of daily life during the summer months across the country, from picnics to pool parties and house parties to pop-up shops.

But even more than that, it has developed into a concrete culture.

It has taken root!

Today, rosé is the fastest growing of all the wine categories and I'm tickled pink.

Regarding my relationship with pink wine, I let go of the judgements and shame and insecurity a long time ago – along

with most of the wine-loving society. I can proudly say that I love to drink rosé wines and I don't care who knows.

Well, that's not exactly true. I very much care who knows.

That is why I wrote this book. I want the world to know – for the record – that I adore rosé wine.

And I'm going to drink it and enjoy it, hashtag, my way – #rosémyway

: the introduction

I emerged from the Columbus Circle subway station, maneuvering past the slow-moving sidewalk traffic with the dexterity and intensity of an Olympic track star.

I was being a typical New Yorker – in a major rush – on my way to the Museum of Art and Design on the Upper West Side of Manhattan. I was attending the first-ever Provence Iconic Panel and Experiential rosé wine tasting sponsored by Vins de Provence.

The beads of sweat danced on my head, ran down my neck and slid down my back.

I was in a state.

The temperature was a mild 71 degrees that day. It was only the 21st of May 2019, a Tuesday to be exact. But I was really feeling the heat.

It was exactly one week away from the release of my very first wine education book called the "The Less is More Approach to Wine."

I was feeling all the feelings: excited, anxious, relieved, nervous, proud and pressured.

Not only had I taken nine full months out of my hectic life to write the book, I was also responsible for the publishing, the public relations, the social media, the launch events and planning the book tour.

While I was extremely excited about my book launch journey, the opportunity of being transported into the world of rosé wine, if only for a few hours, was a welcomed distraction.

After checking in, saying hello to some friends, poking around my swag bag and being led to the auditorium, I eagerly sat down, pulled out my notebook, clicked my pen and prepared for the discussion.

Speaker by speaker. Chart by chart. Topic by Topic. And detail by detail, I found myself taking copious notes – page after page – oftentimes simultaneously merging the information I was taking in with my own thoughts.

Before the two seminar sessions were over, I felt my heart start to race. It seemed I came to a super scary and equally exciting epiphany: I was going to write a second book that was solely about rosé wine and it *had* to come out by the next summer.

This came as a complete shock to me. The thought caused actual heart palpations.

While I was thrilled to have just written my first book – which had not even officially come out yet – I had no idea if the book would be welcomed in the wine world or how the book would be received generally. And now, I was already thinking about working on book number two.

What the world!?!

Then on top of all of that, the process of writing my first book was super intense. It was long, challenging, draining and extremely lonely at times.

Yet, I was exhilarated about the idea and the subject matter. I was euphoric, in fact.

I was really stirred up because this would be a great opportunity to take a closer look at the rosé wine category – from around the world – through my journalism, sommelier, wine educator and consumer lenses.

I would have the chance to produce a much more fleshed out version of rosé education than what I have previously been able to offer during my 90-minute wine classes.

That is the night – Tuesday, May 21, 2019 – when "Maneuvering Rosé Wine with Style" was conceived; in that auditorium and in front of all those people.

That inception laid out my next step as an author, helping me continue the mission of bringing people closer to wine through my education work.

And just like that, I was off to the races; off on a new journey and off on the development of this rosé education book.

: the scope of the book

Rosé is light, fun and festive.

Well, that's generally the consensus among wine lovers, consumers and industry professionals.

It's typically so easy to drink that some people jokingly liken it to a form of "summer water."

Simply saying the word *rosé* can evoke substantial amounts of joy.

And don't bringing a bottle – or several – to a gathering in the summertime. That generous gesture will garner you loads of praise in the form of hugs, kisses, high fives and other joyous declarations.

When framed like that, rosé wine sounds like the best thing ever.

But is that all there is to rosé: light, fun and festive?

What if it didn't go down so easily? What if the word rosé or related hashtags were not so fun to say? What if rosé wasn't the popular, go-to drink of festivities from Memorial Day to Labor Day?

Once the celebrity endorsements go away, the vacation season ends and the temperatures start to drop, what do you have?

Would you be excited about rosé?

Would you drink it?

Would you enjoy it?

As you can see, I have all the questions.

I, however, do not have all the answers.

Those, my friends, are up to you.

Since wine is such a personal experience, we must answer those questions for ourselves.

But I do have information to share that might help you figure out your own unique relationship with rosé.

That's where this book and I come into the picture.

"Maneuvering Rosé Wine with Style" was written as educational tool to shed some much-needed light on this entire category of wine.

I want to empower consumers to make up their own minds about rosé – getting to know it on a more individual level. That goes for both the wine lovers who already embrace this category of wine and the others who have yet to make up their minds.

I've had a front-row seat to the rosé wine industry for some time now as a certified sommelier and wine educator. And, full disclosure, I am a super fan of rosé – personally and professionally.

I know that rosé is extremely popular and extremely misunderstood.

The book's goal is to strip away the hype surrounding rosé and present the heart and soul of a complex wine category that gets underestimated because of its appearance and overshadowed by social situations.

Regardless of if you love rosé or strongly dislike it – hopefully the information in this book helps lead you to a greater overall respect and appreciation of the larger rosé wine category.

: the way to use this book

I model my wine books like I structure my classes.

The objective is to make them fun, easy to understand and a little silly at times.

Therefore, I write in a tone that is very conversational – as if I'm speaking directly to you in a class.

This approach feels comfortable to me as a writer who likes to use a literary, narrative journalism style. Plus, it seemed to go over well in my first book.

We all know wine education can be complicated and intimidating.

Not every topic is going to be so easy to process right way. Therefore, I hope the tone makes some of the less palatable information a little easier to digest.

It will take some time for things to click and for all the dots to connect with wine. Therefore, I use a bit of repetition throughout the book.

You will also find that I provide reference points to specific chapters where more detailed information can be found. These markers serve as "internal indexes" of sorts, in the event you want to refresh your memory on a subject. In some cases, those reference points will indicate that more details are coming a little later in the book for more clarification.

In terms of structure, the chapter flow is linear – for the most part.

The intention was to have each chapter progress into the next for a cohesive, full story. But I organized the book with the rosé wine consumer's interest in mind, while still trying to do the proper job of a wine educator and sommelier.

As a result, I arranged the chapters in an order based on what I perceived was important for the setup of the larger story.

Then I considered what consumers might find more interesting in learning as the book progressed.

I worked to ensure important background was included as part of my wine educator role. I also made sure that practical tips on rosé enjoyment were provided from my certified sommelier experience.

That was my process for writing this book.

But that doesn't necessarily have to be your approach when reading it.

This is for your enjoyment and education. Approach this book anyway you'd like. Each chapter shares a unique perspective and can stand on its own as an educational tool.

Read this book from cover-to-cover. Jump to the chapters that better suit your immediate needs. Or use the book for quick references on rosé wines.

All of that is perfectly fine.

The overarching objective is to provide information that applies to any of those unanswered questions you might have when trying to better understand the rosé category.

Before you decide how you want to dig into the book, however, there are some key things to keep in mind.

The words *rosé* and *pink* will be used interchangeably throughout the book moving forward. These are two popular terms that both refer to this category of wine, so just know that they are one in the same.

Next, there is a section of wine terms found in the back to further help make sense of the information outlined in this book.

Finally, there is a stand-alone chapter on food and wine pairings in relation to rosé wines. You'll understand why this is a significant addition to the book when you get there or skip ahead to that chapter.

Now that you have the "lay of the land," it's time we get started.

I truly hope you find something in this book that is helpful in advancing your understanding of rosé and the broader pink wine category.

Here we go.

Cheers!

CHAPTER ONE: **the pink wine category**

It is trés chic to drink pink.

It really is. Rosé has somehow become the wine du jour in today's world.

But as previously mentioned, that was not always the case.

There was a time, just 25 to 30 years ago, when rosé was not even considered a "true wine" in certain circles.

That viewpoint is pretty puzzling to me since rosé has all the elements that embody a true, classic wine.

It has alcohol, acidity, minerality and a touch of tannins. We'll delve more into those topics when we get into CHAPTER TWO: **the styles and structures**.

However – I suppose – when rosé is viewed and tasted alongside the great red wines of the world, the pink wine category tends to pale in comparison.

That pun was very much intended. Sorry, but I couldn't resist.

Since the "non-wine" perspective has been around for some time now, it appears that the best way to start this chapter is to understand exactly what a rosé wine is and what makes up this overall pink category.

Let's first explore the concept of rosé wine.

Rosé wine is an alcoholic beverage made from the fermented juice of mostly red-skin grape varietals / varieties. These grapes come primarily from the Vitis vinifera grape species with origins around the Mediterranean region.

The skins of the grapes – ranging in red, blue and purple colors – are fermented with the juice for a short duration of time. During that time period, the skins of the grapes offer up a small amount of color.

That juice ends up having a pink-ish color.

However, in select instances, the pink color can also be garnered by the blending of red and white wine together. More on that later.

Next, let us focus on the word "rosé."

Rosé is the primary word associated with wines of this color. It is a French word that translates to "pink" in English.

With France being such a well-respected winemaking county and having its fingerprints all over the wine industry, the general and global term for pink wine is rosé.

Regardless of the region the pink wine comes from – Austria, New Mexico, South Africa, Portugal – the overall term the industry uses to describe these wines and the category is the blanket term "rosé."

That applies to both still / flat wines and sparkling wines that have bubbles.

In terms of learning about rosé, that is the probably the most straight-forward aspect about the wine: pink wines are called rosés and rosés are pink wines.

This is when it starts to get a little confusing, however.

There are a variety of other names within the larger pink wine category – based on regions and winemaking styles – that also refer to these wines.

In addition to rosé, other names include the following: blush, rosado, rosato and vin gris.

The words "rosé" and "pink" can be used interchangeably to refer to these wines in general, but blush, rosado, rosato and vin gris apply to specific styles of these pink wines.

Blush wines are connected to California. Rosado wines are connected to Spain and Portugal. Rosato wines are linked to Italy. Vin Gris is linked to a pale style of rosé primarily from France.

Essentially, these names are linked by the *color* they all have in common. Other elements that link these wines together will be outlined more in CHAPTER TWO: **the styles and structures**.

How we feeling? I know that was a lot to digest so far.

Now that we've set a baseline for understanding the names, styles and the general category, the next thing to peel apart is how this style of wine came into existence.

The pink wine category is deeply rooted in a long, complex and sorted history.

The upcoming sections will call attention to some important historical highlights, links to different regions and illustrate how rosé came to be associated with a more casual, carefree and celebratory lifestyle.

The archives are now open. Let's take a quick peek around.

: the historical perspective

"All roads lead to Rome."

That is an expression you might have come across at some point in your life – maybe in written form, as a spoken proverb or in a Sarah Jessica Parker movie.

It is a loose Latin translation of the statement, *"mille viae ducunt homines per saecula Romam,"* coined by the French poet named Alain de Lille in 1175 A.D., during the European Middle Ages.

While the phrase offers various modern philosophical interpretations like "there are many routes that can be taken to reach a goal" or "several ways to reach a conclusion," it was originally connected to an actual truth of that time period.

The literal translation is "a thousand roads lead a man forever to Rome."

During the Roman Empire's height of power, it covered about two million miles around the Mediterranean region as it ruled over 60 million people for about 500 years. The time frame was officially from 27 B.C. to 476 A.D.

All the roads in various parts of the empire – from the spread-out villages and towns – were constructed by the Roman army to literally link back to the original capital city of Rome.

When it comes to rosé wine and its French origin, that phrase seems quite apropos.

Like many concepts that permeate our world today like democracy, legal systems, city infrastructures, water management and social services, winemaking was explored and further developed under the Roman Empire.

But those practices didn't start there. The genesis of wine – like several other professional fields – pre-date the Roman Empire.

Roman leaders were influenced by several earlier civilizations. Those concepts and contributions to society were then absorbed, tweaked and appropriated by Roman leadership and spread across the empire.

But before we get into the influence of the Romans, let us take a brief look back at life and wine before the start of the empire.

What started out as an "happy accident" in the discovery and production of wine back around the year 10,000 B.C., moved into purposeful production around the year 3,000 B.C.

That new level of wine production coincided with the development of agriculture in Mesopotamia, the Fertile Crescent along the Mediterranean region, with the wine grape species known as Vitis vinifera.

Historians have ascertained that wines at that time were likely fermented from a collection of both red and white grapes. They were picked from the available, nearby vines.

The grapes were blended and left to ferment together, resulting in a lighter style of wine with varied colors.

Many historians believe that the first colors of wine ranged from amber and rose gold to light pink and dark ruby. That was all dependent on the grapes available in the region.

Various civilizations started to develop over time in the region – Sumerians, Babylonians, Assyrians, Canaanites, Phoenicians, Egyptians, Etruscans and Greeks.

They migrated, traveled and eventually settled throughout areas that are now known in today's world as Turkey, Syria, the Republic of Georgia, Armenia, North Africa, Northern Italy and Greece.

These cultures found themselves exploring and crisscrossing the neighboring regions to make new allies by trading information, practices, goods and services.

The Phoenicians – a specific group of Canaanites – began to sail and trade across the Mediterranean region from their initial home in Lebanon, their established colonies and then eventually their new settlement of Carthage in North Africa.

They were selling and trading everything from dye to grapevines.

Two of the most famous trading partners and major benefactors were the Egyptians and the Greeks. Historians suggest the Phoenicians introduced both civilizations to wine sometime between the years 1500 B.C. and 300 B.C. – although it could have been even earlier than that.

The Greek civilizations slowly started to integrate wine into their daily lives and habits. Wine soon became so integral to life that it became a symbol of economic strength to the city-states and the lands they colonized.

As wine became more of an in-demand product from Greece, the Greeks started to share their successful winemaking practices to areas that are now Spain, Southern Italy and Southern France.

Enter southeastern Gaul.

This is a region that would eventually become Provence in a country that would later become known as France.

We'll put a pin in that for now as we continue the story.

A group of Greeks sailors called the Phocaeans started to set up a colony and large-scale trading center in southeastern Gaul. They were from an area called Phocaea in a region that is now mostly Turkey.

They called this colony Massalia – now known as Marseille, France – and settled there around 600 B.C. Shortly after, other nearby cities were created including Antipolis (Antibes), Monoicos (Monaco), Nikaia (Nice) and Athenopolis (Saint-Tropez).

The Phocaeans were credited with planting the Vitis vinifera grape vines in the region sometime after they cultivated the area.

600 B.C.

While other civilizations were producing wine at that time, Greek winemaking was very popular. They had a very interesting approach to wine. Most of those practices, however, haven't stood the test of time like mixing wine with herbs, sea water, spices and other additives to enhance the flavors. Although, for a while, the Romans did incorporate using additives in their wine like honey or cheese.

But what did stand the test of time was the legacy of early Greek winemaking in that region. The Phocaeans were the reason why pink wine would become so closely connected to the region we now know as the South of France.

However, as fate would have it, The Roman Republic – which would evolve into the Roman Empire – entered the picture.

The Phocaeans initially set up an alliance with the Romans around 218 B.C., for protection against nearby threats and invasions. Then – little by little – the Romans started to take over the larger area. The final conquest of Massalia and the neighboring cities occurred between 24 B.C. and 14 B.C.

In 8 B.C., it was a wrap. A monument was erected under the instruction of Emperor Augustus to celebrate the victory, signifying that this was the first section of Gaul ever to become part of the Roman Empire.

Under the Roman Empire, that region was referred to as "Provincia Nostra" – our province. Today, of course, it is known as Provence, France.

Roman control over the region soon shifted into winemaking. The empire took what they learned from the Greeks – and other wine producing civilizations like the Etruscans and Egyptians – and started creating new winemaking techniques.

Those merged and expanded practices paved the way for modern-day wine procedures, including separating the grapes by color and more intense pressing by feet stomping and mechanical wine presses. That helped to produce bolder wines with darker red hues.

As the empire grew, the Romans spread their enhanced knowledge of grape growing, vineyard management and winemaking to other regions under its rule.

The wine culture spread to places across what is now Europe; the rest of Gaul (France), Germania (Germany), Britannia (Britain), Hispania (Spain and Portugal), all of Italy and other nearby locations.

In addition to the Romans spreading a wine culture throughout those areas, they were also spreading a new religion called Christianity.

Once a polytheistic society, Catholicism became the official religion under the empire in 313 A.D., long after the death of Jesus Christ. The rulers eventually created a new Christian capital called Constantinople in the east of the empire, west of Rome.

This religious shift is important to note because it would set the stage for the importance of wine in the world for many cultures around the world.

Under the Roman Empire, the Catholic monks became involved in winemaking as it became engrained in religious practices. It became a symbol for the blood of Jesus Christ. The monks took charge of growing grapes, making wine and planting vineyards throughout the empire to create a healthy supply of sacramental wine.

As the church grew, so did wine production.

And then about one hundred years later, the Roman Empire came to its end after five hundred years of being a massive, regional superpower.

Because of its time in power, the Romans are credited with a slew of contributions to modern-day society. The short list of its legacy includes the concept of democracy, the spread of Christianity and the cultivation and evolution of a wine culture that would last for thousands of years.

In that regard, the poet Alain de Lille's statement – "all roads lead to Rome" – is so true in literal, figurative and historical ways. The empire's influences linger on to this very day throughout several parts of the modern world.

And that influence ties the spread of wine – and specifically pink-colored wine – back to the Roman Empire starting in that section of southern Gaul originally colonized by the Greeks back in 600 B.C.

: the light wines during dark times

The collapse of the empire ushered in some very troubling times that lasted hundreds of years during the Middle Ages.

Much of that time was referred to as the Dark Ages, as the Roman Empire was picked apart by invading, surrounding empires and ruled by new Germanic leaders.

One constant through it all was the Catholic Church. Through their production of wine, the church had acquired a great deal of power, land and influence throughout the region. They were able to pick up the slack of services that were no longer provided under Roman leadership, while also looking out for the physical and spiritual needs of the residents through church services.

Part of that responsibility meant the monks continuing and increasing the production of wine.

After a few hundred years, life settled into its "new normal" under the feudal system – a social hierarchy system for kings, lords, barons, clergy and peasant classes. That structure set up a form of protection, security and normality that had been missing for a long time.

In this new system, wine was now the preferred beverage to drink in areas that were becoming Britain, France, Italy, Germany and Spain.

These wines served to honor Jesus Christ, but also functioned as a healthy source for hydration, medication and socializing.

And it really started to become a unifying force in the region.

There was one pink wine from Bordeaux that had a massive impact on the British. Love was in the glass and the British could not get enough of a deep pink wine from Bordeaux called Clairet.

Clairet was produced in the Graves region of Bordeaux, while other parts of Bordeaux were starting to produce darker, more intense red wines.

This lighter style of Bordeaux wine – most likely a blend of red and white grapes – was deemed less harsh and more enjoyable by the masses.

Its popularity might have also helped bring two kingdoms together.

In 1151, the marriage between French and English nobility – Eleanor of Aquitaine and Henry II – linked the two regions together for about 300 years.

That connection further helped spread the interest in Clairet as Ireland and Scotland also became enamored with these wines through trade efforts.

As to be expected of those everchanging times, tastes, palates and wine styles continued to evolve and change as the Middle Ages progressed into the Renaissance period from the late 1400s to the early 1600s.

There was an increased focus on deeper reds, fortified wines and sparkling wines to pair with the population's renewed interest in classical art, music and culture.

Lush red wines were being produced in the Burgundy region in the north using the Pinot Noir grape and Gamay for a while. Heavier, darker reds were coming out of Bordeaux, in the form of Clarets (not to be confused with the dark pink Clairets) using the Malbec,

Cabernet Sauvignon, Merlot, Cabernet France, Petit Verdot and Carménère grapes.

We'll get into some of those more in CHAPTER THREE: **the grapes**.

With this new thirst for bolder wines, it appeared the interest in pink wines were starting to decline.

However, with the official incorporation of Provence into the Kingdom of France in 1486, pink wines were not quite out of the game just yet.

That event allowed for the region to continue evolving its traditional winemaking practices in the south. And like Bordeaux and Burgundy, Provençal wines had acquired its fair share of fans.

There was a group of naval officers from Marseille that formed the Knights of Medusa between 1683 and 1690. It is a brotherhood group of Bacchus – the Roman God of Wine – that is still in existence today. Their main objective was, and still is, to celebrate their love of Provençal wine and food through fellowship and the art of living well.

While there was a dedicated devotion to these wines in the south of France, things were different for pink wines outside of Provence.

Pink wines were slowly but surely getting eclipsed by the popularity of other growing wine styles.

Like in Champagne, for example.

This region in northern France first started out as a region that produced dark pink wines. However, it wasn't out of desire. It was out of pure circumstance.

The monks were still leading the charge in wine production from the local abbeys around France. Under their control, wine production flourished into a full-fledge enterprise for the church.

In hopes of capitalizing on the members of the royal court and bourgeoisie in nearby Paris, The Benedictine monks in Champagne were trying to compete with Burgundy to sell wine to that market.

They were trying hard to produce red wines like the popular and well-respected reds that came out of Burgundy. That, unfortunately, wasn't possible primarily because of the terroir and climate issues in Champagne. We'll get into those topics more in CHAPTER FOUR: **the place**.

With Burgundy being a tab bit further south than Champagne, the wine producing regions were warmer. Therefore, the grapes were able to ripen more during the growing season. That resulted in the production of fuller red wines – full in the context of what a Pinot Noir grape can produce.

Using Pinot Noir grapes, the winemakers in Champagne decided to work with their cooler climate limitations, utilizing their existing knowledge to make something unique.

Initially, they went in a different direction and sought to make a richer white wine, using red-skin grapes. The monks tried the saignée method – a bleeding method – in winemaking. Unfortunately, they didn't have the science down just yet.

The wines turned out to be somewhat pink in color.

This style eventually worked out in the end because it became rather popular in Champagne. It was called Oeil-de-Perdrix. It's a French phrase referring to the pink and copper color of the eye of the partridge bird. This style of wine also gained notoriety – through production and consumption – in nearby Switzerland.

While Champagne couldn't complete with the Burgundy for red wines in the Parisian market, it would eventually find its niche with the development of a sparkling wine.

These, now famous, bubbly wines became popular with French elite and royalty in 1715. By 1764 – using the saignée method – the Champagne House Ruinart was documented as producing the world's first rosé Champagne.

Control of wine production was now shifting in Europe.

As the power of the increasingly fragmented Catholic Church decreased over time, winemaking control began transitioning to a négociant system comprised of noble families, landowners and private business owners.

Once the French Revolution occurred in 1789, that uprising ensured that any remaining vineyards belonging to the church were completely broken up and sold.

Private entities started creating wines under their own names and labels to keep the tradition of winemaking moving forward.

But they did it on their own terms.

Pink wine would consequently fall out of the consciousness of many winemakers throughout France.

The expanding wine markets were demanding different styles of wine from the more highly regarded regions.

Before long, the overall pink wine category, and its French origin in Provence, was out of sight and out of mind.

: the beautiful age

Provence had really been through the wringer.

After being occupied by Greeks, Romans, Christians, Barbarians, Arabs, Spanish and the French, the region had faced a series of extreme highs and lows.

It was battered by war, devasted by a plague and practically neglected by most of France by the late 1700s.

The region was viewed as a backwater, underdeveloped rural fishing village that was inconveniently inaccessible to most people in Paris and other parts of France.

Therefore, it continued to stay out of sight and out of mind.

Through it all, however, Provence managed to solidify a distinctive cultural identity; a strong regional personality with an appreciation for the simple things in life.

Over time, the residents made use of their local treasures and many artisanal industries started to grow there. There was everything from perfume to textiles, olive oil production and pottery making, and, of course, winemaking.

Then things started to change. The outside world was beginning to take notice of Provence.

Word was beginning to spread about this sunny place near the sea. There was intrigue building about this land full of vineyards, grape vines, olive trees, lavender fields and seafood.

By the late 1800s, the British upper class soon found themselves descending upon Provence in droves, taking respite from the dark, dreary winters in England.

After the British settled in, they helped shepherd in a time that was later referred to as "The Belle Époque" – the good times or the beautiful age.

It also established a new industry for Provence: tourism.

By the end of the 1800s, the larger region was referred to as the Cote d'Azur (the Blue Coast), also known as the French Riviera.

The completion of railway projects helped make the region more accessible to visitors. It soon morphed into a popular tourism destination for the European noble classes – Russian aristocrats, British royalty, French nobility – and industry magnates.

This time, more specifically from 1871 to 1914, encapsulated a luxurious sun-kissed era full of warmth, pleasure, leisure and escapism during the winter months for the European upper class.

They were infusing the region with wealth, luxuries, infrastructure and architecture.

Then the artists came. They were attracted to the blue skies, blue water, bright colored flowers, landscapes and sunshine.

The region served as inspiration for several famous names like Paul Cézanne, Auguste Renoir, Marc Chagall, Vincent Van Gogh, Henri Matisse and Pablo Picasso.

They were infusing the region with art, beauty and culture.

Vacationers absorbed the unique delicacies of the region – seafood, fresh vegetables, flowers, perfume, sun, coastline and wine of various colors.

Provence had seemingly grown out of those rough, rugged awkward years and stepped into its own renaissance of sorts.

There was the creation of great art, great literature, great architecture and great socializing.

Everything seemed so quaint, calm and peaceful.

Then a little bug came and caused mass destruction to vineyards, putting a major damper on the party.

Phylloxera is a small, microscopic bug that feeds on the roots and leaves of grape vines leaving them starved for water and nutrients. The bugs were unknowingly transported to areas throughout Europe from the United States of America around 1866. Within a few years, they destroyed about 70 percent of Europe's vineyards by 1870.

The devastation forever eradicated many popular grape varietals grown throughout parts of Europe, particularly in southern France.

It was an extremely difficult time for winemakers.

Many producers were slow to rebuild and replant. When they did, the focus shifted to lesser used grapes, like Carignan for example in the south of France. These grapes were not considered ideal, stand-alone grapes to produce wine. But they helped winemakers garner higher yields to bounce back faster.

One young man from Alsace – in northeastern France – saw potential in Provence where many people just saw a problem.

Marcel Ott used the opportunity to buy up land – which was cheaper after the Phylloxera spread – and worked to rebuild several estates in the Provence region with a handful of available grapes.

Winemakers during this time were infusing the region with a new style of high-quality, signature rosé wines.

: the lure of sunshine

The sun was on its way to shine on the wine industry again in Provence.

Vineyards were starting to recuperate. The region was expanding. More tourists were coming.

Then another major shift in life occurred. This time it was one that would forever change the landscape and structure of the world.

That was the first world war.

For four years, from 1914 to 1918, the "world" powers battled each other. By the time it concluded, it left so many lasting effects.

In parts of Europe, there was mass destruction, frustration and change. The war brought down many of the royal houses in Europe that were previously in place.

That helped lead to the creation of a new world economy, propping up the U.S. as a major power on the new world stage.

It also supplied the U.S. with great wealth, which was beneficial for many of its citizens as well.

Money and power created an overall sense of joy in the U.S. by the 1920s. It was a joy that also lead to a great deal of excess in the form of crime, nightlife, jazz, alcohol and wine for select populations at that time.

Those individuals – ranging from successful American business leaders to high-profile celebrities – took their celebrations to Europe and found a sunny, happy place in which to play in the South of France.

With Americans mixing it up with European celebrities like Coco Chanel and Picasso, the two groups were instrumental in shifting the vacation period away from "wintering" to "summering" in the South of France.

It was like a "new beautiful age." Provence was an ideal destination for warmth, pleasure, leisure, simple sophistication and escapism, this time for the summer months.

As the rich and famous across Europe and the United States descended on the French Riviera "en masse," a lifestyle and culture was being cemented.

Drinking up the lush life of hot days, warm nights and chilled pink wine became synonymous with Provence and the French Riviera.

The rosé of choice at that time was Domaine Ott. After purchasing several estates and producing high-quality rosé in the late 1800s, the company caused a must-have demand in the 1930s when it created a distinctive glass bottle modeled after the amphora clay drinking vessels of ancient civilizations.

It wasn't long until the South of France gained a whole new set of visitors – outside of the elite, wealthy classes.

New French labor laws increased its citizen's salaries and provided them with paid vacation starting in 1936. That milestone – along with a new railroad system – provided city individuals and families an up-close-and-personal look at the sophistication and serenity of the region. It was their first taste of regional delicacies like aioli, bouillabaisse and the new Provençal rosés.

And just like that, the world was at war with itself again.

The second world war started in 1939, bringing in a five-year conflict that would continue to push forward change.

After that major conflict, the U.S. was officially established as a major superpower in the world. Europe was forced to build a more unified political and global identity. And by the mid 1900s, the world collectively was trying to move into a new and different mindset.

: the global rosé fascination

There was a new thirst for life.

The second war was over in 1945.

The life altering and dark days of war were officially in the past – at least in terms of physical conflict.

Countries around the world were looking for things to pull them out of that those past experiences: economic depression, devastation and destruction.

The focus shifted to science, technology, manufacturing, film, television, economic growth, travel and developments in winemaking.

And, of course, rosé was a perfect distraction.

The rosé industry in Provence was still growing and evolving. Those who could afford to, flocked to the French Riviera after the second war.

A slew of Americans flocked to the French Riviera. Artists and writers flocked to the French Riviera. Actors and actresses flocked to the French Riviera.

In fact, an entire film industry flocked to the French Riviera in 1946 when Hollywood started to attend the annual Cannes Film Festival.

People wanted warmth, pleasure, leisure and simple sophistication. It was the ideal place for people to leave their personal cares and worries behind.

Rosé was engrained into the fabric of the Provençal culture in the South of France. More and more producers were making serious efforts to make better wines from high-quality grapes.

Some of those wines even found themselves being exported to select areas around the world, like Domaine Ott, offering up a taste of Provence in a bottle.

Since not everyone could physically enjoy the spoils of Provence or in a bottle by proxy, other winemakers found creative ways to offer up some pink wine joy to the world.

Right after the war ended, two Portuguese companies decided to throw their hat into the rosé wine ring under the Mateus and Lancers brands.

These wines, however, were set apart from the Provence styles by their higher sweetness levels and slight effervescence.

Receiving a warm welcome in the Northern European and U.S. markets, the Mateus brand accounted for about 40 percent of Portugal's export sales in the 1950s, selling more than 3 million cases per year.

This style of semi-sweet pink wine would so popular that it helped pave the way for another style of wine that would enter the picture about 30 years later.

As the world became more connected, wine production and the wine world expanded.

Companies were starting to produce wines for more discerning national and international wine markets, propping up France and Italy as the "gold standards" for wines around the world.

The U.S. was producing wine too. However, the country was in a precarious situation. Several years after the war, the industry was still rebuilding from the effects of Prohibition, the 18th Constitutional Amendment that prohibited the sale and consumption of alcohol from 1920 to 1933.

Wine was only legally produced and consumed for medicinal and sacramental purposes during that time. Although the ban only lasted 13 years, it led to vineyards either being replaced by other crops or left completely abandoned.

From the 1950s to the 1970s, winemakers around the world continued getting more and more serious about producing better quality wines.

The U.S. was only able to start to rebound by the 1960s, surviving on the production of bulk and jug wines as a primary source of revenue. And like the U.S., other winemakers in regions like South America and Australia were focused on the tried-and-true techniques of respected regions like Bordeaux and Burgundy in France.

With all eyes on parts of Europe as a source for the finer things in in life like wine, food and culture, pink wines were once again being regulated to the fringes of the wine world.

These New World wine countries – regions outside of Europe – were working to apply new knowledge to improve their own production of red and white wine, looking to become "gold standards" in their respective regions.

As time went on, the global wine world started to become increasingly fragmented. Some producers held tight to tradition while some new producers opted to rebel from the restrictions of tradition, resulting in evolving styles in both the Old and New World wine regions.

The winemakers, who were empowered by a certain level of freedom, made it their mission to carve out their own individual paths through experimentation, innovation and forward thinking by the late 1960s.

Then the '70s showed up.

: the case for white zinfandel

White Zinfandel.

Yes, we are going there.

Those two words evoke a variety of mixed emotions whenever this wine happens to present itself in a social setting or in a conversation.

Whether you happily embrace it or cringe at the sight of it, White Zinfandel created a seismic shift in wine consumption overall in the U.S., bringing fresh attention to the pink wine category.

The story of White Zinfandel is another happy accident in the wine world.

It is a fascinating story that speaks to the universal forces surrounding winemaking and the entrepreneurial mind of American winemakers.

In the United States, the major focus of winemaking was on red and white wine at that time. It didn't have the cachet of France or Italy. But there was a large demand for wine in the country and winemakers in California were working hard to fulfill that need.

The way that need was met was to produce inexpensive, jug wines made in bulk.

White wine was the preferred wine of the moment. With advancements in temperature controlled, stainless-steel fermentation tanks around 1964, winemakers were making white wines that were clean, fresh and approachable.

But there were not enough white grapes to keep up with market demands in California and the U.S.

As a result, many of the winemakers turned to their red grapes for the juice until they were able to plant and grow more white grape varietals.

In order to achieve the lighter color style of wines from the red grapes, they utilized the saignée method to bleed the juice from the grapes – a more advanced approach than what the Champagne and Swiss winemakers used in the 1700s.

Like the wines made by French and Swiss winemakers, the wines would turn out to be light to medium pink in color. In fact, it was suggested that these pink wines in California be called Oeil-de-Perdrix, after the style created in Europe. But the U.S. governing body of wine, the Federal Bureau of Alcohol, Tobacco and Firearms, rejected the suggestion. Instead, the wines were referred to as "white" versions of their red grape names.

As a result, the names White Zinfandel, White Merlot and White Cabernet Sauvignon were used to try to appeal to white wine drinkers.

That all started around 1972. However, these wines from California would forever change the pink wine category in 1975.

The winemaker for Sutter Home in Napa Valley, Bob Trinchero, was making this new style of "white wine" from the red Zinfandel grape when he encountered a problem during the fermentation process.

He decided to add some juice from the Mission grape to the batch of Zinfandel and the wine stopped fermenting. It was stuck. The yeast stopped eating the sugar in the juice to bring it to full fermentation. That stuck fermentation also left a generous amount of residual sugar in the wine.

After a few weeks of careful consideration, tasting the wine and not wanting to waste money nor wine, Trinchero decided to release this new version to the market.

It was a bit of a departure from the White Zinfandel wines released by Sutter Home a few years earlier because those were drier pink wines.

To everyone's surprise, customers loved it.

It was almost like the Mateus and Lancer wines from Portugal, except without the fizz.

The company's first release was made from about two thousand gallons of wine which quickly sold out. By 1980, the company had sold a total of 24,000 cases of this new White Zinfandel.

By the 40-year anniversary of the release of this style of Sutter Home White Zinfandel in 2015, the company had made more than 6 billion dollars in sales with an average of 3 million-plus cases sold every year.

This naturally disrupted the California wine market. Other local winemakers were inspired to make their own "white" versions from Zinfandel, Merlot and Cabernet Sauvignon.

With the wide range of styles and producers, these wines were turning into its own, full-fledged category.

In 1978, winemaker Charles Kreck coined and trademarked the word "blush." After conversing with wine writer Jerry Mead about the word, Kreck felt it perfectly summed up these styles of pink wines hailing from California. The two things that distinguish this blush style from other pink wines is that it typically represents an American pink wine that is either off dry or semi-sweet.

While the blush category received a large amount of fanfare from many consumers, these wines were met with a certain level of distain by the industry.

These pink wines seemed to be taking the California wine industry in a different direction than most winemakers wanted to go.

Americans were getting super serious about its wine and wine production.

After beating out French winemakers in a blind wine tasting challenge called "The Paris Wine Tasting of 1976," Napa winemakers were known for making some of the best Chardonnay and Cabernet Sauvignon wines in the world.

These winemakers sought to continue taking their winemaking game to the next level and that sentiment had a ripple effect with other winemakers globally.

Investments and efforts were being poured into making world-class red and white wines that spoke to a region's terroir and highlighted the skill of its winemaking team.

Pink wines were just not thought of as world class – at least, not at that time.

: **the great rosé surprise**

The time for rosé to shine would finally come.

However, there was no clear indication that this would happen.

For decades upon decades, rosé wine merely existed in the shadow of the red, white and even sparkling wine categories.

Now rosé wine is everywhere.

Capturing the interest of consumers and the respect of wine critics, rosés are now considered world-class wines.

The demand around the world is real and it is documented.

Let's check a few receipts.

The year 2018 was a milestone year for rosé.

The global consumption of rosé went from 18.3 million hectolitres in 2002 to 25.6 million hectolitres in 2018.

The nearly 26 million hectolitres comes to more than 300 million bottles of pink wine.

That spike represents a 40 percent increase over a 16-year period.

This is all according to the 2020 "Rosé Wines World Tracking: Confirmations and New trends!" study conducted by CIVP/FranceAgriMer – Dowel Strategie. The organization compiled, analyzed and disseminated data on the production and consumption of rosé wines in 47 countries from 2002 to 2018.

Those figures are even more impressive considering the news that overall wine consumption had declined in 2019 for the first time after 25 years of continuous growth. That's according to the global alcohol tracker, IWSR Drinks Market Analysis.

The tables had turned. Rosé was now outpacing the growth of the two major wine categories.

It probably comes as no surprise that France had a major role to play in this achievement.

The country is both the largest consumer and producer of rosé wine – with Provence as the leading rosé producing region in France, generating about 150 million bottles in 2018.

There is such high demand for pink wines hailing from that region that about 90 percent of wines from Provence are rosé wines. And throughout all of France, one out of every three bottles consumed is a bottle of rosé.

While France's role in these numbers is not shocking, what's particularly interesting are the United States' numbers.

The U.S. is both the second largest producer and consumer of rosé wine – outpacing classic winemaking regions like Spain and Italy.

Blush wines like White Zinfandel still make up a large volume of pink wine consumption in the U.S. However, the dry styles – specifically – the Provençal rosés reached a high of 2 million cases purchased in the U.S. by 2018, according to Business France, a French government agency.

That number represents a major shift in consumer behavior considering that there were just about 123,000 cases of rosé from Provence in the U.S. market in 2008.

: **the rise of rosé**

Not even Nostradamus – the famous physician, astrologer and self-proclaimed prophet who was born in Provence in 1503 – could have predicted the unexpected rise in popularity of rosé.

For some, these numbers are exciting. And, for others, the numbers may seem quite appalling.

Overall, this paradigm shift came as quite a surprise to most people who consume wine.

Yet here we are.

But, exactly how did we get here?

For 45 years, since 1975 to 2020, the change was slow and subtle through a series of fortunate events for rosé.

It seems the success of rosé has potentially revolved around four key factors – travel, celebrity, savvy businesspeople and wine influencers.

Let's explore these possibilities.

First, you have the world travelers.

Rosé has long been a must-have beverage for those who have traveled to Europe, particularly to parts of the South of France.

A nice cold glass of rosé was the perfect remedy for the searing heat of the Provence sun and the perfect accompaniment for the Provençal cuisine.

It's just what you do there. It's kind of like the "when in Rome, do as the Romans do" mentality.

The wine captivated a mix of people from celebrities and chefs to moguls and tastemakers.

These individuals had the power and influence to spread the gospel about these pink wines from Provence – and the lifestyle it represented – to anyone and everyone who would listen.

Eventually these wines slowly started making their way around the world.

Provence rosé were being served in fine-dining establishments and Michelin starred restaurants in places like Beverly Hills – the sister city to Cannes, France. Then it started showing up on menus in restaurants in big cities like San Francisco, Miami, New York City. Rosé also made a grand showing in hotspots like the Hamptons, the popular summer destination for affluent NYC residents.

As the visibility of rosé increased and its consumption became more acceptable, wine companies – producers and distributors – were more than happy to feed the demand.

Some winemakers increased their pink wine offerings by reducing their red wine production. Some companies expanded production through vineyard acquisitions. And more rosé on the market allowed importers and distributors to expanding their product portfolios in select markets around the world.

When the warm weather months come around, the practice of "summering" and sipping on rosé became intertwined with each other far outside of the confines of Provence.

It became the ideal summertime swill for world travelers and the jet-set crowd.

It was perfectly light and fun. And it proved festive enough for all the summer activities like picnics, pool parties, barbeques and, of course, the major summer holidays.

Then came the power of celebrity.

They were moved to evangelize their enchantment with these wines in several different ways.

Either through perfectly posed photos on social media or launching their own wine brands, celebrities helped push Provençal styles of rosé into the spotlight and into mainstream society.

For the everyday wine consumer, rosé was a win-win. The wines were delicious, high-quality wines from France at affordable prices. The wines can be found typically for $20 or less per bottle.

That was it. The match was struck. The fire was lit.

All that helped fuel the strong burning desire and demand for rosé wine – reaching a fever pitch around 2010.

Rosé was now big business and businesspeople want a piece of the pie.

Nearly every summer after that point on, there was a new pink wine being sold either by a new company, by a different celebrity or in a new type of packaging.

The category was increasingly getting more attention from the media, with headlines in the *New York Times* and the *New York Post* to *Wine Enthusiast* and *Food & Wine Magazine*.

More pink products and more media attention brought more and more fans.

Social media influencers and clever brands collectively moved the needle on the awareness of these pink wines. Those efforts took the category to a celebrity-like status of its own.

Campaigns went viral. Memorable hashtags were created. Pretty pictures of happy people drinking up the summer were canvased all over social media pages.

The Provençal summer lifestyle of "The Belle Époque" and the Cote d'Azur were striking a connection with the young – and not so young – drinkers. Not only was it acceptable to drink rosé, it was almost unavoidable in social settings.

Consumers were being presented with countless ways in which to develop a personal relationship with rosé. There were new wine classes, food and wine pairing events, grand tastings, rosé-themed picnics, cruises, festivals and even a rosé mansion experience in New York City inspired by the world's fascination with the wines.

It was official.

Unexpectedly, the pink wine category emerged from a niche, summer vacation wine to one of the most celebrated styles of today's modern wine world.

: **the future of rosé**

The rosé bubble has yet to burst.

The U.S. volume of rosé imports is projected to reach 3 million cases by 2020, which would continue to set record highs in terms of sales and consumption.

Experts are even projecting continued growth in the category through 2035, with nearly a 20 percent increase in production. That would result in about 30 million hectoliters of rosé being produced globally.

If these industry predictions come true, the pink wine category craze has no clear end in sight.

That is big news.

But it also raises some big questions for the future: What are some things to be excited about? What are some things to be on the fence about? And what are some things to be concerned about?

Exploring these questions can reveal some possible good news, display some uncertainty about the future and unfortunately expose some potentially bad news for the world of rosé wine.

I'm a "let's go with the good news first" type of person, so let's start with what I consider to be the "good news" related to the future of rosé wines.

: the potential good news

There is a lot to be excited about related to the future of pink wine.

At the core of that excitement is the concept of "change."

Overall, the wine market has been changed dramatically because of the popularity of rosé.

In many instances, we can thank the winemakers of Provence for that.

This style has been the major game charger in the category. As an industry leader, it has pushed wine, wine-related concepts and the category into exciting new directions.

The changes can pave the way for the continual evolution of products within the pink wine category and other themes that extend far beyond it.

Let's get into the general groupings of these contributions and changes.

: the major shifts

Rosé now has respect in the industry.

Consumers, experts, the culinary world, and the wine media have developed a strong respect for these wines.

That is allowing for more styles within Provence to garner continued respect.

It also allows for a diverse group of other pink wine styles to be taken seriously as well – from different colors, to different regions, to different flavors and different textures.

That respect is opening the door for more growth in terms of pink wine production and consumption in the U.S., China, Australia, South Africa, Canada and the United Kingdom.

It is also inspiring other countries to get deeper into the pink wine game. As a result, there could be several unique offerings coming from places like Austria, Hungary, Romania, Chile, Argentina and Switzerland.

Consumption habits have also shifted, particularly in parts of the the U.S.

Pink wines were once mostly regulated to the spring and summer months. The sales typically were from April to August. Now there are more stores and restaurants stocking, selling and serving rosé wines all year long.

Rosé wines are now finding a permanent place at the winter holiday parties and dinners.

This "war of the rosé wines" competitive market has also inspired some companies to step up their game.

That competition has even given new life to styles like White Zinfandel from California and Mateus from Portugal. Traditionally these wines are sweet pink wines. Now Mateus and White Zin producers are experimenting with dry styles to attract a new type of consumer.

The success of pink wines is not only inspiring professionals inside of the category, its influence is spilling over into the beer and spirit industries.

Major liquor and beer manufacturers are now producing pink vodka, pink cider, pink beer and pink tequila.

With big brands pouring resources into the "drink pink" craze and the "pink lifestyle," those efforts could provide continued unintentional support to the growth of rosé wines for several years to come.

: the forward-thinking innovation

The pink wine category has also really shaken up the wine world with innovative packaging.

On the store shelves – in retail settings and online – rosé wines are being featured in a variety of new packaging options. In select markets, you can find BPA-free plastic PET wine bottles, cans of wine in various sizes, boxed wines in various sizes, kegs and even new wine pouches hitting the market.

Embracing these alternative packages styles can help push the tried-and-true traditional wine producers globally to think inside the box or the can or the pouch or the plastic bottle to adapt to changing lifestyles and behaviors.

The keg might be a little too much of a push for them at this point. We'll have to wait and see about that one.

Then there are the different bottle shapes.

Savvy rosé wine producers have capitalized on the concept of pink wines not being taken too seriously in the industry and have opted for more adventurous bottle packaging.

The options seem to evolve more and more every year. These new bottle types include perfume-like bottles, square bottles, etched glass bottles, carved glass bottles.

Then those bottles are adorned with beautifully designed patterns that range from minimalistic art touches on the labels to mural-like bottle coverings.

Some pink wine producers, however, do want to be taken more seriously.

They want to produce the next great rosé wine that customers want to collect and keep for a while.

Therefore, there is a chance, in the next 5 to 10 years, that Provençal winemakers might introduce a new style of rosé; a style that can potentially age and mature over a 10-year period.

The going philosophy, currently, is to drink rosé wines within one or two years of its vintage.

That means most consumers are drinking a very young, fresh wine. Wine stores have even been mapping out their buying of rosé wines to ensure their inventory is sold by the end of summer, making room for the next year's vintage the following spring.

Experimenting with the idea of rosé wines that are meant to be laid down and aged until they reach their ideal time to drink could shift the way consumers and stores view these wines.

The narrative can shift that rosé wines don't have to be only consumed when they are young.

If the execution of this concept works it could add another layer of validity to pink wine being a real, formidable wine category.

: the environmental concerns

One of the most exciting benefits the pink wine category has consciously pushed forward – particularly from the Provence region – is the commitment to organic farming and sustainable vineyard practices.

The Provence winemaking region has its eyes closely fixed on the effects of global warming. They look at how it effects the growing season, the grapes and the annual harvests.

To protect this superstar rosé producing region, Provençal winemakers, scientist and government officials are looking at the future to determine how they can sustain it for the long term.

That involves potentially focusing on existing, or approving new, grape varietals that can better withstand these changing temperatures.

It also includes shifting to mostly organic farming practices to protect the land and its biodiversity, moving toward a universal organic farming program throughout the region.

In terms of sustainability, it involves them looking at how they can tweak winemaking practices to do a better job of reducing waste, limiting water and electricity use, and decreasing glass bottle manufacturing by instituting bottle recycling programs for the wineries.

There seems to be some real thought and investment put into keeping the pink wine category alive, from the region that's the currently leading the market.

I'm sure others in the industry will follow suit.

: the uncertainties

Just a heads up, this section might come off a little like an *SNL* "Debbie Downer" segment just without the tears of laughter.

With the possible increase in rosé production globally, it does bring up some concerning questions.

Too much of a good thing is not always a great thing.

Rosé wine is now on the map. Provence is the leading region. It's a leading wine category with some clout and power. And it's bringing in a fair share of currency from around the world to the wine industry.

That has brought increased competition, a potential strain on natural resources and a larger number of selections customers can choose from.

Please forgive me in advance for the highly probable awkward probing. But there are some potential issues that could arise as the category grows.

: the consumer confusion

The region of Provence has become *the place* to get quality rosé wine. That wine style has somewhat become the poster child of what a good rosé should embody. That has in turn caused a lot of imitation of sorts that is not completely flattering.

This classic "dry, pale style" that Provence has become intrinsically linked to in the hearts and minds of consumers, is starting to pop up in places around the world – catching the attention of consumers who are looking for a type or a specific color.

Some wine producers, in their respective parts of the world, have opted to make this "type" of rosé to secure a share of money spent in the pink wine category.

While it is a producer's prerogative to select any shade in which to make their rosé, it can muddy the rosé waters a bit in terms of wine being a product of its environment.

Wine – in its historic sense – is meant to express the characteristics of a region or the land's terroir.

If the focus becomes shopping for a color as opposed to the region, it strips away the importance of the land it comes from. This is important for die-hard wine lovers. It also becomes confusing for the general customer.

I can lead many consumers to think that all rosé wines are essentially the same. Then the notion is to shop for a rosé in their price range that is dry and a certain shade of pink, regardless of the regional contributions.

: the celebrity saturation

Don't get me wrong.

I love celebrities. I know a few. I consider some of them to be my friends.

I love to watch their films. I love to read their books. I love the way they make me laugh, think and dream.

And, in some cases, I love their wine.

You can just feel the "but" coming, right?

But, the recent onslaught of celebrity wine producers can further overshadow some of the inherently unique traits of pink wines that make them special.

This is a hot wine category that is continuing to rise in consumer spending and production. There is also a lot of freedom to innovate and be creative within the category.

That would make the pink wine category attractive to any celebrity who is business savvy and investing in their financial futures and that of their families.

It's just that the list seems to get longer and longer each year.

The concern is that it is yet another layer that overshadows the wine – its history, its connection to a place and the professionals working the land and producing the wine.

Quality rosé wines can potentially lose much of the footing it has gained over the last 20-plus years by putting more focus on who is associated with the wine rather than a quality of the juice in the bottle.

And I'm not suggesting that celebrity owned wine companies or branding agreements are a bad thing or that they do not care about the nuances of wine.

I happen to enjoy some of these brands because they are extremely delicious wines – not because of the person's name on the bottle.

And who knows?

Maybe one day, I'll become a celebrity and decide I want to produce a wine.

It can happen. Dreams sometimes do come true. I watch Oprah's "Super Soul Sundays." I'm a believer in the Law of Attraction.

I'm just contemplating the pros and the cons. It could serve as a double-edged sword.

On one hand, these wines can capture the attention of new customers and the millennials who have been slow to embrace wine over the last few years.

It appears that their lack of interest in wines has helped lead to the first recent decline in growth in the wine industry in 25 years. Reports show that these younger drinkers have been opting for spirits, beer, ciders and other types of specialty, mixed alcoholic beverages.

This could "influence" them to try wine for the first time or give wine another chance. In that sense, that is wonderful.

However, on the other hand it can help undo all the work that has been done over the years to raise rosé to a respectable standard in wine by oversaturating the market with celebrity brands.

This is what I'm on the fence about in terms of the future of rosé.

With the increasing global competition and ever-growing list of celebrity-owned brands, will the pink wine category take several steps back in its progress by becoming a flat, one-dimensional group of wines with little else going for them but their pretty color or by which celebrity owns or licenses the brand?

: the potential bad news

Everything must change.

What goes up comes back down.

Palates change. Lifestyles change. Interests change.

It's just the reality of life.

What happens to the rosé category as things start to change in the next five to 10 years?

Provence is producing most of the rosé wines that the world is consuming right now. However, Provence is a small region.

There has been a lot of attention on the area in the last 20 years. The wine real estate in that part of France is mostly all under some type of ownership.

There is no physical way to expand the production capabilities in Provence, except to potentially stop making red and white wine and become solely a pink winemaking region.

At some point in the future, their production capabilities will be maxed out. There are only so many natural resources to go around to produce wine.

What happens then?

Perhaps Provence can sustain its leadership role in the industry, but how does that play out in terms of supply and demand?

Will that mean that the prices will keep going up? Will an affordable, high-quality Provençal rosé under $20 be a thing of the past?

Then there are changing consumer mindsets.

We as consumers can be very fickle.

What's cool now could become passé in a few years.

Is it possible that classic rosé will one day get the White Zinfandel reaction when you bring it to a party?

Will it go back to living in the shadow of red and white wine options?

Or will it be one of those things that you only drink when you visit the south of France or other summertime destination while you soak up the sun and refresh your palate?

I am not a fortune teller nor am I a new world Nostradamus.

I'm just a curious wine professional.

Only time will tell us how the future of rosé plays out.

One thing I know for sure is that *now* is the ideal time to *really* explore rosé.

Because one day down the road, you might decide the explore the options more only to find out that you missed the ideal window of opportunity. I really hope that won't be the case. But only time will tell.

CHAPTER TWO: **the styles and structures**

Picking the topic for this chapter was quite the challenge for me.

I'm being completely honest. When organizing the flow of this entire book, the struggle was real.

Much like telling a story, I like to write pieces that have a clear beginning, middle and end. That's also typically how I structure the wine classes I teach in NYC, online and throughout the country.

Personally, that's just the easiest way for me to learn. I like to have information laid out in a liner fashion. However, I decided to go in a different direction with this book.

Before segueing into the details about the "place" where grapes grow and the actual grapes used to make pink wine, I decided to tackle a more pressing matter.

There is this tightly confined box that pink wines have been regulated to by legions of consumers, winemakers and even many wine experts.

That box is the "style."

One main style of rosé has become the singular focus in the wine industry: pale, light, dry, crisp and French.

Folks have been enamored with this typical "Provençal style" of rosé for some time now, even if it doesn't come from Provence.

There are growing numbers of winemakers around the world trying to emulate this style as consumer dollars create a high demand for it and elevate its popularity.

That popularity has done – what I believe to be – somewhat of a disservice to this pink wine category.

This tunnel vision pursuit for a very specific style has caused a homogeneity or sameness within the pink category that unfortunately excludes a large range of other distinctive textures, colors and flavors.

As a result, this archetypal style has unintentionally made the category seem fairly one dimensional to wine consumers.

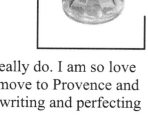

But rosé is not a one-note samba. It is not lacking depth. And it is most certainly not a one-trick pony.

Pale, light, dry, crisp and French are all wonderful and amazing attributes. But it does not represent all pink wines.

And please don't get me wrong.

I love, love, love Provençal rosé wines. I really do. I am so love drunk when it comes to them that I might move to Provence and live out my older days teaching, drinking, writing and perfecting my garlic aioli technique.

The popularity of rosé, led by the Provence styles, is the one of the main reasons I chose this topic as my second book.

It is because I am such a big admirer of these pink French wines that I feel compelled to educate wine consumers about the different styles produced throughout Provence.

Provençal rosé wines are not strictly confined to pale, light, dry and crisp.

There is amazing diversity in Provençal rosé wines.

They can embody several distinctive styles using various grape combinations – resulting in wines that are fresh and light to those that are bold and savory.

Focusing on one singular style of rosé – pale, light, dry, crisp – can distract you from a large pool of options with attributes that might be better suited for your palate.

That can prove problematic in an overall understanding of pink wines.

It's almost like putting the focal point solely on looks when being attracted to a person. There's a chance you might pass up a better match that is highly intelligent, hardworking, funny and a great cook.

That's just an example, not that I'm specially referring to my life or any personal experiences.

Then outside of Provence, there is a whole big world of rosé out there just waiting to be explored.

It is a full-fledge wine category that has layers and nuances and depth. Don't limit yourself to just one style within it.

Try the different colors, body types, aromas and distinct flavors from within Provence and around the world.

And that, my friends, is why I decided to focus on the styles and structures for the second chapter in the book.

I wanted to impart a clearer perspective of the entire rosé wine category, working to showcase the beautiful diversity of rosé for all the readers to see.

Maybe it will get a few readers to think outside that pale, light, dry, crisp, French rosé box and have a lot more fun in this pink wine world.

: the styles of rosé

I admit, I use the word style a lot.

It falls out of my mouth all the time. It happens so much that people probably think it is my all-time favorite word.

It's not my favorite word, for the record.

I have a few choice four-letter words that I'm quite fond of like "wine" and "food."

But "style" does have a certain *je ne sais quoi* (I don't know what) quality to it when referring to wine categories, wine consumption and the wine lifestyle.

This five-letter word – when used as a noun or a verb – has a great way of succinctly summing up a slew of topics associated with the elements of wine and wine education. Yet it speaks volumes when showcasing the broad range of options and various connotations.

Rosé wine has all the styles.

There are still styles and sparkling styles of rosé.

There are lighter styles and there are heavier styles.

There are light-pink styles and there are dark-pink styles.

There are dry styles and there are sweet styles.

There are young, fresh styles and there are aged, mature styles.

And those are only few examples to consider.

Then we can bring up the regional styles. We'll get more into that in CHAPTER FOUR: **the place**.

Then finally, in terms of style, there comes that personal connection with the wine. That feeds into your personal style. This is when you determine if the wine's characteristics align or not with your personal tastes and individual preferences. That will be addressed more in CHAPTER FIVE: **the personal palate.**

Like I stated before, rosé wine has *all the styles*.

There is so much to dissect.

For now, we will delve first into how rosé is made and how the styles and structures unfold from that process.

: the still rosé production

Rosé! Rosado! Rosato! Blush! Vin gris! Pink!

These are the names that make up the pink wine category that has been on nearly everybody's lips lately.

This is the rosé wine world and we're just living in it.

For some, it is the wine that summers have been waiting for. For others, it is the wine that food has been waiting for. Then there are the others who cannot wait for this whole craze to be over.

Wherever a person falls on the spectrum in their loving or loathing of pink wine, it is very important to get a firm understanding about the category before we commit to a certain stance.

That starts with how pink wines are made.

Unlike its red and white counterparts, pink wine requires a different – often more painstaking – production process. That goes for both the still and sparkling rosé productions found around the world.

Like red wine, rosé is made from grapes that have red, blue or purple skins. Therefore, in order to make a wine that falls into the pink category, you will need red skin grapes – regardless of the process and where the wine is made.

When it comes to wine, in general, there are always exceptions to the rule. Rosé is no different.

rosé
rosado
rosato
blush
vin gris
pink

We'll get into those "exceptions" a little later. But for now, we will focus on the rosé wine production made from red grapes to produce still, non-sparkling wines.

The Vitis vinifera grapes are most commonly used in traditional winemaking. That is because everything is contained in and on the grapes that is needed for the fermentation process – converting the grapes into wine.

Those essentials are yeast, sugar and skins. The yeast is found on the grape skins and the sugars (mainly fructose and glucose) are found inside the grapes. And the skins of the grape will offer the wines a wide range of coloring – depending on the style being produced.

Wine fermentation happens when yeast on the skins – or any added cultivated yeast – interact with the sugars in the grapes. When the grapes are pressed and crushed, the yeast cells from the skins are now physically introduced to the sugar in the juice. The yeast will then eat the sugar, creating heat through this metabolic activity while also converting the sugar into alcohol.

> **yeast + sugar = alcohol (ethanol) and carbon dioxide**

There is a byproduct that is also produced during the fermentation process called carbon dioxide (CO_2). However, the carbon dioxide blows off the fermenting wine and into the atmosphere during the primary / first fermentation stage.

Lastly – at least for this part of the process – the skins are left to sit and soak with the juice of the grapes. The color from the skins begin to seep into the juice for a short period of time.

And this is when the rosé party officially begins. As we say in New Orleans, "laissez les bons temps rouler" (let the good times roll).

Just to reiterate, this is how still, non-sparkling rosé wines are made. This process is referred to as the primary alcoholic fermentation – the same process of red and orange wine (white wine grapes fermented with skin contact).

This process also creates the base for sparkling wines. We'll get to that a little later. At this moment, we will focus on pink still wine.

Here are a handful of methods winemakers can use to achieve rosé wine after the fermentation process has started.

Limited maceration — After being pressed and crushed, the skins, seeds and juice only sit together for a short amount of time to achieve a light bleed of coloring. That time frame is most commonly between 2 and 72 hours in stainless steel tanks or a neutral oak vessel. Two to six hours of skin contact creates a light-colored wine. Around 24 to 48 hours, you have a wine that has deeper, darker tones. Some winemakers will opt for a little longer skin to juice contact for longer than two days. It is important to note that darker rosé wines are not automatically sweeter. These wines will offer more body with longer skin contact but will still fall on the dry wine spectrum – unless the winemaker opts to purposely make the wine sweet or semi-sweet.

Saignée method — (**salasso** in Italian, **sangrado** in Spanish) — This is a method that produces a rosé wine as a byproduct of red wine production. Saignée means "bleeding" in French. While

producing a red wine, winemakers will bleed off a portion of the juice. This portion will be lighter red in color as the wine hasn't spent much time soaking with the skins. This method happens early in the winemaking process. The typical goal for this method has been to concentrate the texture, flavors and structure of the red wines being produced. Therefore, this method produces two different wines, a bold red version and a rosé version.

Vin gris — This style of rosé production uses a press where the juice and skin barely interact. There is no maceration time between the juice and the skins. With that minimal interaction, there is very little bleed of color that gets into the wine. Therefore, the color of the wine is so pale that it sometimes looks like a white wine or very pale rosé. But the wine made from red-skin grapes.

Blending — This could cause some confusion when learning about pink wines. That is because the word "blending" has two very important meanings in the wine industry. While blending a variety of red-skin grapes is very common in some of the most popular rosé wine regions of the world, this method involves the blending of red and white grapes together to create a pink-colored wine. While many people might initially think this is the primary way of producing a rosé wine, this process has been mostly limited to sparkling wine options around the world and some still wines made in countries outside of Europe.

While outlining these rosé making methods, there were a couple of fermentation vessel concepts that worked their way into the copy.

To clarify a bit, in order to ferment a wine, you will need a vessel to contain it. Therefore, it's an extremely important part of the winemaking process.

There are four major vessels used today to make wine: oak barrels, stainless-steel tanks, clay pots and concrete eggs. Winemakers can use one vessel solely or opt to use a combination of these vessels for their winemaking purposes for any type of wine, including rosé.

Oak barrels – also known as barriques – have unique abilities to allow wine to develop, soften, absorb flavor and age rosé wine over time. Wine barrels can feature *neutral* oak barrels for fermentation and storage purposes. These are barrels that have not been treated by fire on the inside. These types of barrels don't give off any major flavoring to the wine, except maybe damp wood. Because of its porous nature, the barrels allow for the gradual influx of oxygen. The flow of air can both soften structures in the wines and make the wine more concentrated through evaporation. This vessel style is usually associated with rosé wines that are either a little richer or the ones that are meant to lay down and cellar for years.

Stainless-steel tanks – also known as stainless-steel vats – are large, neutral vessels used to ferment wines. Being a neutral vessel, these tanks don't offer any flavoring or coloring to the wine. The tanks allow the essence and integrity of the grape to stay intact and shine through in the wine. With them being temperature-controlled, stainless-steel tanks allow winemakers to have more control over the fermentation process. Since the tanks are easy to clean and maintain, the vats also help insure fresher, cleaner wine by preventing bacteria from spoiling wine and avoiding off-putting smells. The result is a more aromatic, bright wine.

Clay pots have been used in winemaking from the Neolithic period by ancient civilizations in China, Egypt, Greece, North Africa, Armenia, the Republic of Georgia and at the beginning of the Roman Empire. With the popularity of the "natural wine" movement, new styles of clay pots are making a comeback among a handful of Old and New World winemakers. While the term "amphora" is used commonly to describe the pots, other names like tinajas and dolia – to name a few – represent more specific styles and shapes of these clay pots. The most common style is called kveri / qvevri that has been used for about eight thousand years in Georgia. Many modern-day winemakers are experimenting with new styles of clay pot fermentation for some of its "natural" rosé wine offerings.

Concrete eggs tanks are modern-day, off-shoots of clay pots. These new temperature-controlled, egg tanks are used by many winemakers in California and other parts of the world. This style is more similar in makeup to the clay pots, but also features some of the same benefits oak and stainless-steel fermenters offer. The concrete wall keeps the wines cool and can also control the fermentation. The eggs also allow small amounts of oxygen to interact with the wine like oak barrels, but don't offer any flavoring to the wine like stainless-steel tanks and traditional clay pots. Many of these, like the clay pots, are used in the production of "natural" rosé wines.

Before we pop the top off the rosé sparkling production, we will take a little time to bask in the range of colors and the nuances of the aromas these wines offer up as a result of the various production methods.

: the skins

Under the watchful eye of skilled winemakers, these red grapes – with various nuances of reds, blues and purples – can be guided to emit some of the most beautiful shades of pink you'd ever see outside of a Pantone color chart.

There are so many unique shades for rosé wine: pale-pale pink, pale pink, onion skin, rose water, rose gold, salmon, dark pink and medium ruby.

It's clearly the first thing a person sees.

What people can also see – through a little "guesstimation" – is how long the skins and the juice had to soak together, or macerate, in order to achieve its color.

As we learned earlier, a rosé wine is primarily made from red skin grapes when the grape is pressed and crushed and left to sit together for a short period of time.

The time can range from winemaker to winemaker based on the preferred rosé color they want to achieve. But the duration of time is generally anywhere between 2 to 72 hours. In this regard, I am referring to the limited maceration pressing.

Then with the Vin Gris style, there is very short contact. When the grapes are pressed, the juice immediately goes into one container and the skins are left behind in another container. For the saignée method, the juice is often deeper pink or light red because the juice is pulled off from the juice of a red wine.

The shorter the juice-to-skin contact time, the lighter the pink color. The more time the skins hangout with the juice, the more concentrated and deeper the color will be.

Here are some timeframes and corresponding colors to consider.

- No maceration time (Vin gris style): super pale, faint hint of pink
- 2 to 6 hours of contact: pale pink, peach, onion skin, rose water
- 6 to 12 hours of contact: rose gold, pale salmon, copper, medium pink
- 12 to 24 hours of contact: salmon, light coral, hibiscus, maraschino cherry
- 24 to 72-plus hours contact: light ruby, cherry, raspberry, burgundy

The two- to six-hour mark is typically representative of the pale, light, dry, crisp Provençal style. Whereas, some rosé wines in the six- to 24-hour maceration period are more in line with the standard Cote du Rhône, Spanish, Portugal, South African and some California styles. And the styles that macerate for more than 24 hours tend to fall into a natural wine style or rosé wines that are meant to age for an extended time period.

There is another important thing to know about the final color of a rosé wine. The final color isn't solely achieved from this skin to juice contact. For wines made from multiple varietals, each varietal goes those that maceration process separately and then the winemaker blends them together. This helps them achieve the final taste and final color.

Lastly, I must address the Pink Elephant in the room.

There is a big misconception about the sweetness levels of deeper, darker-pink rosé wines. The darker rosé styles are misinterpreted by wine consumers to always taste sweet. The color of the rosé has no connection with the sugar level of the rosé.

We'll get to sugar levels coming up later in this chapter – for still and sparkling wines. But since we're on the topic of the color, I wanted to clarify that point. I get asked that all the time in my wine classes.

The maceration time that skin and juice have together is what determines the color, besides the mixing of multi-varietal rosé wines. After the duration is over, the wine is left to continue to ferment. It's at that time, the winemaker can either let all the sugar ferment out of the wine or allow for some residual sugar to be left in the wine.

Therefore, it's not the color of the wine that connects a rosé with a sweet or dry style. It's the fermentation choices of the winemaker.

: the aromas

Smelling a wine is half of the fun of tasting it.

When you smell rosé – of course, after you swirl it around first – you should be presented with an array of scents and aromas that float from the glass.

Those scents could be an assortment of items like peaches, strawberries, melon, salt, honey, spice or Earth. The grape varietals, region, fermentation vessels and winemaking techniques will dictate the exact nuances you are smelling.

Although these are grapes, when fermented they take on different chemical compounds that are shared with other things, like flowers and herbs and citrus for example.

Dr. Ann C. Noble, a sensory chemist and retired enology professor from the University of California at Davis (UC Davis) took a scientific approach that best describes the smells found in wine. That led her to develop the Aroma Wheel. She related the specific chemical formulas associated with scents in wines and associate them with the common nouns we use on a regular basis. Therefore, it's a matter of using your sense of smell while layering it with your words to describe what you are smelling in the glass.

Aromas can also be shaped by the age of the wine. When a rosé wine is younger, it offers up more fresh fruit notes from sour to fruity. Then as wine ages – which happens to some rosé wines – those fresh fruit notes tend to turn into more concentrated notes of aged fruit, like a fruit that is almost past its prime or a fruit that has been dried like a cranberry, strawberry or cherry.

Pink wines will also have a distinctive smell that sets them apart from both red and white wines, although there could be some similarities that cross over from time to time.

: **the rosé sparkling wines**

This style is most definitely pretty in pink.

It's shimmery. It's sparkly. It's luxurious. It's fancy.

Having a glass of sparkling rosé makes me feel like I have a nice chunk of change in bank, like I'm in an episode of "The Lifestyles of the Rich and Famous." Then I soon realize there's not much money left in the bank because I just bought a bunch of these sparkling rosé wines.

I digress.

The sparkling rosé is a style of wine that has bubbles in it caused by trapped carbon dioxide.

Some people call it bubbly wine. Some people call it fizzy wine. But the general category across the board – from around the world – is called sparkling wine.

That is what separates the still rosé wines from the sparkling rosé options: the bubbles.

It's like giggles in a glass because the bubbles can tickle your nose, making the situation feel just a little more special.

Keep in mind that in order to make a sparkling wine, first a still, non-sparkling wine is made. Then the CO_2 is trapped in the wine during the secondary fermentation process which provides the bubbles.

The base wines will normally be produced from red grapes or a combination of red and white grapes.

: the carbon dioxide

We have gone through that traditional alcoholic fermentation a few times. Once the process starts, it creates heat, carbon dioxide and alcohol.

During the first fermentation process, we lose the carbon dioxide. In order to capture the carbon dioxide, the wine must undergo a secondary fermentation initiated by the winemaker. There are a few different ways to accomplish that, but let's understand a little bit more about what the carbon dioxide does to the wine.

Carbon dioxide, CO_2, is a colorless, odorless gas consisting of one-part carbon and two parts oxygen. It is produced by burning carbon and organic compounds and by respiration. It is naturally present in air and is absorbed by plants in photosynthesis.

When the CO_2 is trapped in the wine it created bubbles, but also a considerable amount of pressure. That pressure can be quite a lot in sparkling wines. It has been measured as the equivalent of two car tires, as high as 6 or 7 atmospheres of pressure or it can be as low as 1 to 3 atmospheres of pressure.

Sparkling wines that are fermented in the bottle tend to have a high amount of pressure, making the bubbles in the wine more intense. And some other methods of sparkling wine production, can produce milder carbonation which leads to the CO_2 escaping from the wine faster.

: the sparkling rosé wine types

To make a sparkling wine that is pink, the winemaker will, for the most part, make two wines – one red wine and one white wine.

Remember that section about blending?

This is the process that involves blending the fermented juice of a red wine with that of a white wine to produce a variety of sparkling rosés from around the world.

The white wine will be used as part of the base wine, maybe 50 to 90 percent of the wine. Then a smaller ratio of red wine will be mixed in with the white wine for flavor, and of course, to garner the rosé color.

Just like a pink wine can be called a variety of names based on its style and region, there are specific names for sparkling wines from different regions.

Without a doubt, the most famous style of sparkling wine is called Champagne. This style comes from specific regions in Champagne, France. A pink sparkling wine from this region would be called a rosé Champagne.

Then there are sparkling wines made in France, but outside of Champagne, France. Those are primarily called a rosé Crémant. In the South of France, other names can apply like either rosé Blanquette de Limoux or a rosé Mousseux.

In Spain, these sparkling wines are called rosado Cava.

Italy has a lot of sparkling wine options throughout the country. The word "spumante" is the Italian word for "sparkling." In the Veneto region of Italy, these wines are mostly called a rosato spumante or rosato Prosecco. In Lombardy you have rosato Franciacorta. Then a rosato Lambrusco sparkling wine is produced in Emilia-Romano.

In Germany and Austria, the sparkling wine is called a either rosa or rosé *Sekt*.

In South Africa, the category is called a rosé Cap Classique.

And, again, the words "sparkling wine" serve as a general catch-all for other wines with bubbles.

The wines can be Brut, Extra Dry and Demi-Sec, which dictate the sugar level in the sparkling wine category.

This brings us to the dry versus sweet discussion. There will be more details in an upcoming section related to still wines, however, generally dryness in wines means a lack of sugar across both categories.

A wine with little or no sugar in the juice is considered dry. Still wines with some residual sugar can range from off-dry to semi-sweet. Then wines with a lot of residual sugar would be considered sweet.

As with some other subjects in the wine world, this concept is counterintuitive. When "dry" in still wines means little to no sugar, the word "dry" in sparkling wine represents more sugar.

Historically, sparkling wines were a lot sweeter in the 1700 and early 1800s than they are today. That was because of taste preferences and preservation needs. The Brut category was invented between

Sparkling Wine Dryness Levels

BRUT NATURE / BRUT ZERO — This can have up to 3 grams of residual sugar per liter.

EXTRA BRUT — The residual sugar tops off at about 6 grams of residual sugar per liter.

BRUT — This category represents wines with 7 to 12 grams of residual sugar per liter.

EXTRA DRY — Extra Dry has 13 to 17 grams of residual sugar per liter.

SEC — Also called "dry," this style has 18 to 32 grams of residual sugar.

DEMI-SEC — This category has between 33 and 50 grams of residual sugar in the wine.

DOUX — The sweetest of them all, the doux category can have 50-plus grams of residual sugar.

1846 and 1854 by the Champagne house, Perrier-Jouët. That has become and remains the standard dryness designation for dry sparkling wines on the market. Sparkling wines have different residual sugar levels amounts than still, non-sparkling wines to differentiate dry from sweet. See the Sparkling Wine Dryness Level chart for more specifics.

: the sparkling rosé wine production

At this point, here is what we know about rosé sparkling wines.

- Sparkling wines feature captured carbon dioxide that provides them with bubbles
- Rosé sparkling wines are primarily blends of red and white grapes to achieve the color and flavor
- The most popular sparkling wine is Champagne from Champagne, France
- Sparkling wines can be made from all over the world

Now it is time to get into the actual production process.

The secondary fermentation can happen in individual bottles or in a large Stainless-Steel tank. The bottle method is referred to as the Méthode Champenoise / Champagne method or Method Traditional / Método tradicional. The Stainless-Steel tank method is called the Charmat method or simply the tank method. And lastly there is the ancient method of making sparkling wine dating back to the 1500s.

Here are the specific methods in more detail.

THE MÉTHODE CHAMPENOISE – The leading secondary fermentation style is associated with Champagne winemakers. It has been crafted over hundreds of years of trial and error. It is called the **méthode champenoise** (Champagne method) or the **método tradicional** (traditional method). This is simply a secondary fermentation that occurs within each individual bottle of sparkling wine – regardless of what region or country the wine is being produced.

In order to create any sparkling wine, there must be a base wine that has been made. The base wine can be made from one specific grape or a blend of grapes. It can also be the same wine from a blend of different years or vintages. The winemaker then adds a mixture of wine, yeast and sugar to the base wine and caps the bottle with a crown cap, like those used on beer bottles. While in the bottle, the yeast will eat the sugar and the secondary fermentation begins. The process creates heat and adds alcohol and carbon dioxide to the wine, which is now trapped in each individual bottle.

This method requires a few more steps before this style of sparkling wine is complete.

Riddling / remuage – The bottles are then placed on a riddling rack to rest at a 35- to 45-degree angle. The winemaker then has a person, team or machine softly twist the wine bottles a little every day for three months or up to one full year. That allows the yeast cells, which have flavor components, to integrate well with the wine. It also shakes off sediment from the sides of the bottles. This process is called riddling or remuage in French. The end goal is to make sure the yeast cells rest in the neck of the bottle.

Disgorgement – To remove the dead yeast cells from the bottle, the winemaker dips the neck of the bottle into a brine solution at temperatures below the freezing mark (-16 degrees Fahrenheit) or they use liquid nitrogen. Once the liquid in the neck quickly freezes, the winemaker turns the bottle right-side-up and pops off the crown cap. The pressure from the bubbles in the bottle pushes out the frozen sediment full of dead yeast cells.

Dosage – To finish off this process, the wine is then topped off – in most cases – with a wine and sugar mixture to achieve the winemaker's ideal dryness or sweetness level. This process is called the dosage. The levels can range from Brut Zero to Doux. See Sparkling wine dryness level chart for additional details.

After the desired dryness or sweetness level is achieved by the dosage, the bottles are then sealed off with a mushroom cap, a wire cage and left to rest on their sides in the wine cellar until the bottles mature and are ready to hit the market.

Wines that undergo this style of in-the-bottle fermentation include rosé Champagne, rosé Crémant, rosado Cava, rosato Franciacorta and pink sparkling wines from many other regions around the world like Germany, South Africa and the United States.

CHARMAT METHOD – Another popular way of triggering the secondary fermentation in sparkling wine is called the Charmat method or the tank method. This process was started by an Italian inventor, Federico Martinotti, who developed and patented his original idea in 1895. Then the concept was finalized by French inventor Eugène Charmat in the early 1900s. The method might carry the name of the French inventor, but the process is tied to sparkling wine made mostly in Italy. Like the traditional method, a base wine must first be created. The wine can be made from one grape or a blend of regional grapes. The base wine is put into a large Stainless-steel tank that is pressurized. The winemaker then adds a mixture of wine, yeast and sugar to the base wine, which kicks off the secondary fermentation. The tank is sealed, and the carbon dioxide is trapped in the wine. The yeast is filtered out. The wine is bottled. These wines rest very briefly, then they are released into the market. Sparkling wines that are fermented in the tank tend to have high to moderate amounts of pressure in the bottle, from 4 to 6 atmospheres of pressure. These styles can be quite bubbly. Then there are also styles that fall between 1 and 3 atmospheres of pressure. These wines are considered slightly effervescent or fizzy; **frizzante** in Italian or **pétillant** in French.

Wines made in this style typically come from Italy in the form of Prosecco and Lambrusco. But this method is also used for affordable sparkling wines from the United States, Germany and other places around the world.

: the vintages

The word vintage can be a little confusing in the wine world.

It can mean one thing for still wines and have a slightly different connotation for sparkling wines. In general, vintage is the year that the grapes for the wine were harvested.

But it is an important distinction for consumers to know, particularly when shopping for either one of these styles of sparkling wine – regardless of the color.

> **Non-Vintage sparkling wine** – The majority of sparkling wines from around the world are in the form of non-vintage sparkling wines. A vintage is the year a wine was made. A non-vintage sparkling wine is produced when winemakers blend multiple vintages of wines together – reserve wine with a fresh vintage – to create their signature house style of sparkling. The style is more consistent from year-to-year due to the blending of multiple vintages.

> **Vintage sparkling wine** – In select cases, sparkling wine will have a vintage if it is deemed by a governing body that a specific year was ideal for growing grapes. When that happens, the winemakers will only use grapes from one particular year to make the sparkling wine. That, therefore, makes it a vintage sparkling wine. This practice of producing "vintage" wines is associated with sparkling wines from around the world. However, vintage sparkling wines are rarer and regarded to be better quality than their

non-vintage counterparts. As a result, they will also be more expensive. A perfect example of vintage Champagne is Dom Pérignon, the prestige cuvee from Moët & Chandon. The Dom Pérignon brand only produces vintage Champagnes and consequently is rarer, more expensive and highly regarded. Since 1921 until now, the brand has only made about 42 vintage Champagnes from very specific years.

METHOD ANCESTRAL – The steps that separate the ancestor method from the Champagne method is that there are no disgorgement and dosage processes. Therefore, the wine is left with its sediment / yeast cells in the bottle and there is no additional wine and sugar mixture added to set a desired dryness or sweetness level.

Basically, halfway through the fermentation process in a larger vat, the wine is added to individual bottles and sealed off with a cap. The wine continues to ferment in the bottle, capturing the carbon dioxide, therefore producing the bubbles. Since these do not undergo the disgorgement process, these wines are technically unfiltered and have traces of yeast sediment. The pressure in the bottle varies on these types of wines. Some can get up to 4 atmospheres of pressure, while many tend to be fizzy, frizzante or pétillant in style.

The South of France is reported to have been where monks discovered that still wine can turn into sparkling wine back in 1531. That is 107 years before Dom Pérignon was even born and tasked to work on sparkling wines made in Champagne. This version is said to have been the world's first sparkling wine – or at least the first documented source of it. And in keeping with that heritage and legacy, select sparkling winemakers have continued to create wines in this style. Although, the method is said to have evolved a bit over time.

Wines that undergo this style of winemaking can come from areas in France like Jura, Loire Valley and Limoux. But there are many winemakers from Italy, Slovenia and parts of the United States, from California to New York, producing these styles. This style tends to coincide with the slow wine or natural wine movement. Under that movement, many of these styles are referred to as Pét-Nats (Pétillant Natural) wines.

: the structures of rosé wine

We started out the chapter looking at the broader scope of the styles of pink wines while I was standing on my "style" soap box.

In the upcoming sections, we'll fill in the blanks a bit more by looking at the individual structures that make up these styles.

Before I get off my soap box in a few moments, I want to be very clear. These are the elements that make wine an actual wine.

If a person calls into question if a rosé is a "real wine," structurally speaking the answer to that question is: "yes, rosé is a real wine."

Alright, I just stepped off my soapbox so we can continue.

At the core, all wines will have the overall structures – alcohol, acid, minerals and tannins. But the structures, and related elements, can vary depending a bit on the style of wine.

We've got a lot to cover, so we'll just dive right in.

: the yeast

Yeast is a single-celled microorganism that feeds on sugar and simple carbohydrates. Most of us are familiar with the concept of yeast when it comes to bread and maybe even beer.

Yeast is abundant in the atmosphere. It floats around us all the time. It lands on the skins in the vineyard where the grapes grow. You might have noticed while shopping for grapes – regardless of the color – that they have a powder-like substance on the skins. If you haven't noticed it before, you will the next time you visit a grocery store, farmers market or vineyard. That yeast on the skins is called the "bloom."

The fermentation can be sparked by wild, native "ambient yeast" found in the vineyard that land on the grape skins. These types of yeast help provide wines with more "terroir" or a sense of place in the wine. However, winemakers can opt to use "cultured yeast" for a more controlled fermentation. This yeast species is **Saccharomyces cerevisiae or S. cerevisiae**. It can also be called budding yeast, brewer's yeast or bakers' years used to ferment beer, bread, chocolate and spirits.

: the sugar

The reason grapes are ideal for wine is because they are high in sugar content from two primarily sources: fructose and glucose. These sugars allow wines to ferment into a desired amount of alcohol.

A dry rosé wine – still or sparkling – means the absence of sugar. Little or no residual sugar can be found in the wine. The opposite of a dry wine is a sweet wine when referring to "table wines" or wines you would have with food.

Sparkling wines have a different set of dry to sweet rules as outlined in the Sparkling Wine Dryness Levels chart.

Dry wines and sweet wines are the bookends for table wines. From dry heading to the sweet side, you have wines that are "off dry" with a little residual sugar and "semi sweet / demi sec" in the middle before arriving at sweet. A dry wine can have less than 10 grams per liter of residual sugar, while a sweet wine can weigh in close to 30 grams per liter of residual sugar. This is all attained through the fermentation process.

Looking ahead to CHAPTER FOUR: **the place**, we will learn that grapes can grow to be under ripe or very ripe. That ripeness level affects the sugar content. Less sugar in the grapes will result in lower alcohol in the wine if the yeasts finishes it all. A riper grape, bursting with sugar, will turn into a wine with a higher level of alcohol and, in some cases, some residual sugar if the yeast can't finish it all off.

: the alcohol

Alcohol is truly an important structure in wine. It is literally what separates wine from grape juice. The average alcohol for wines is between 12 and 14 percent. That is referred to as the alcohol by volume (ABV). Remember that this an average. You will find some wines with an alcohol content as low as 5 percent and some rosé wines as high as 15 percent. Also, don't forget that alcohol and sugar are linked. The sugar is turned into alcohol in the wine. When the yeast eats the sugar and converts it to alcohol, all the sugar can be consumed to achieve a higher percentage of alcohol or some sugar can be left unfermented in the wine in the form of residual sugar. When we look at a wine bottle with a 5, 8 or 10 percent alcohol content, we are looking at a rosé wine that is going to be on the sweeter side. These wines have a decent amount of sugar that was not eaten by the yeast. On the opposite spectrum, bottles with an ABV of 12 to 15 percent have very little or no residual sugar left in the wine. That makes those "dry rosé wines."

: the body of wine

The body of the wine – the texture, the viscosity – is an element that people really respond to but sometimes have a difficult time putting those tactile feelings into words.

Rosé wines can fall into all three bodies styles: light, medium and full. That's dependent on the grape, winemaking style and aging of the rosé. Consumers tend to be more acquainted with the lighter bodied styles.

Essentially, the body of the wine is the weight and the texture of the wine on your palate. In the wine world, we tend to liken the body of wine to the body (weight and texture) of milk. We use the comparisons of skim milk, 1- and 2-percent milk and whole milk. It makes sense to do that since most people have had exposure to milk in their lives at some point.

Light body – Starting off with light-bodied wines, we liken the weight and texture of these wines to the weight and texture of skim milk. It is very light and lean on your palate. Those options would be associated with wines with low- to low-to-moderate alcohol levels.

Medium body – Medium-bodied wines are more closely associated with 1- or 2-percent milk. Now, I don't expect everyone to know the varying degrees of the textures of milk from skim to 1- and 2-percent milk to whole milk. I am still trying to get better acquainted with the milk alternative textures. But a 1- or 2-percent milk is not as thin as skim milk and not as rich as whole milk, so it falls right between those two as a point of reference. The alcohol will be more moderate in scope for these wines.

Full body – Full-bodied wines have a generous amount of weight and texture to them. We liken that body of wine to the body of whole milk. There's a lot more richness and viscosity there. Those wines would represent wines that have a generous volume of alcohol.

: the acid / acidity

Acidity is an important structure in wine that is not often as appreciated as alcohol, but it is very important for rosé wines. It is a key factor in maintaining the quality of the wine by helping to preserve its freshness over time. There are three major acids found in wine: citric acid like what is found in citrus fruits, malic acid like what is found in green apples and tartaric acid found in grapes.

In the cooler climate regions, let's say like Champagne, for example, the grapes that grow there will oftentimes grow to be under ripe or just barely ripe. That is based on the general cool climate of northern France. Given that the grapes are under ripe or barely ripe, the grapes develop and maintain a high level of acid and not a lot of natural sugar.

In very specific terms, outside of the normal conversation about acid in wines, in goes back to the pH level in the grapes. The initials pH stands for "power of hydrogen." The pH is the measure

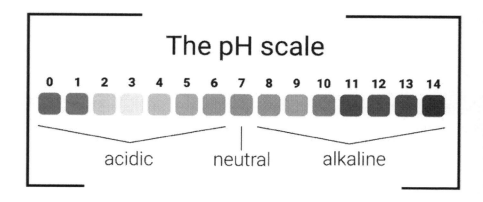

of the molar concentration of hydrogen ions in a substance. That's basically the level of acid or alkalinity – a chemical measurement of a water's ability to neutralize acids – of a solution. The scale ranges are from 0 to 14.

Like with the example of the dryness levels of sparkling wines, there are some concepts related to wine that are counterintuitive or contrary to our common-sense thinking.

The pH level scale is also counterintuitive. Items with ranges below 7 are acidic solutions. Items with ranges of 8 or higher are considered alkaline.

For example, lemon juice, vinegar and wine all come in under 4 on the scale: 2 for lemon juice, 2.2 for vinegar and 2.9 to 4 for wine. Then water comes in at 7, which is neutral, while the chemical lye comes in at 13 on the scale.

As the pH scale indicates, all wines have acid, from a high level to a moderate level. We really don't want a wine to have a low-acid content because the wine will come across as lifeless and flat on the palate. When a wine touches your palate, it has a fresh, mouth cleansing quality. Since all wine has acid, that makes food and wine such a great combination. The wine works to either complement or contrast the dish, while the acid does the heavy lifting of cleansing your palate and getting you prepared for your next bite of food and next sip of wine.

Traditionally sparkling wines, by far, have the highest acid levels. These wines are ideal to either serve as an aperitif or throughout the dinner.

Before a meal, the acid cleanses your palate of any previous items you've tasted like gum or coffee. Then the acid makes your mouth water or "salivate," which sparks your digestive system and make you hungry.

On the palate, higher acid rosé wines tend to be sharp, tart and tangy. Moderate-acid wines come off as a bit softer on the palate, more mellow. And moderate-minus acid wines feel smooth and creamy on the palate.

: the minerals / minerality

Minerality in wine is associated with the smell and taste of elements connected with the Earth's ground. That consists of rocks that are wet and / or have been crushed, metals, salinity, dirt and soil. When you analyze the soil a bit deeper, you can see it can include traces of calcium, nitrogen, potassium, magnesium and sulfur. These minerals play a major role in the health, wellness and productivity of the grape vines.

There are specific soil types in vineyards around the world. The types include things like chalk, clay, limestone, flint, schist, gravel, volcanic ash, sand and loam just to name a few. Each type plays a crucial role in the health, wellness and productivity of the grape vines.

These materials can also include terms ranging from alluvial and calcareous to loam and marl, which can consist of a mixture of several soil types. All rocks are made from some type of minerals. Therefore, soils that are abundant in minerals tend to allow more complex aromas and flavors to develop when the grapes are turned into wine.

The soil helps bring out certain types of "minerality" in the wine, the essence of minerals in the taste and smell of wine. These types of soils are important to the vineyard because they properly nurture the vines all year round – helped by the minerals, nutrients, acids, salt deposits, proteins, nitrogen, carbon as well as the microbiological activity within the soil.

In terms of understanding minerality on the palate, think of it this way. Vines from around the world grow in their own unique soils. The roots of the vines dig deep into the soil and access all the mineral characteristics of that individual plot. The minerals are therefore imparted into grapes on the vines and the minerals from the grapes are imparted into the wine.

When you smell a wine, it might remind of you of wet rocks near a beach or a lake or other body of water. Smelling that allows you to pre-taste the minerality in that wine through your sense of smell.

I'm sure about you, but it's not my jam to go licking on rocks. But if that's your thing, please enjoy yourself.

In other words, you do not have to go licking on rocks to understand what that tastes like. We do about 80 percent of our tasting happens through our nose, therefore you can taste the minerality in the wine without ever having physically tasted a rock.

: the tannins

You have all probably had this experience before with red wine. You've taken a sip and instantly you feel your mouth start to dry out. It's very real. It is tactile. You can feel it when it hits your palate. Sensations can feel like cotton balls, gauze or sand in your mouth.

Those are tannins.

Tannins are chemical compounds, polyphenols, that have a natural astringency to them in liquid. Tannins are found in the skin, stems and seeds of grapes. When the tannins meet your palate via the wine, your mouth will dry out and feel dehydrated to varying degrees.

The juice of red wines has a longer interaction with the skins and therefore develop a prominent tannin structure. Rosé wine, however, will have a small amount of tannins, depending on how long the juice sits with the skins.

In the wine world, tannins are grouped into three major strength categories: soft (low), moderate (medium) and firm (high).

Rosé wines will offer up either soft tannins that have a mild drying out quality on your palate or moderate tannins that have a medium drying effect.

Tannins are also a natural preservative. This structure is instrumental in giving pink wines a longer shelf life. The more tannic structure it has, typically the longer it will age well over time.

: the sulfites

I really hate to be the bearer of what some people might consider "bad news," but structurally all wines have sulfites.

And consumers should be glad that they do.

All wines have sulfites

Sulfites are sulfur-based compounds that are a natural part of the fermentation process. Yeast produce detectable amounts of sulfites when it converts the sugar from grapes into alcohol. While sulfites occur naturally in wine, the compounds are also added to wine in some cases as preservatives. To help slow down the oxidation of wines that lead to the browning and spoiling of the wine, sulfites are typically added at higher levels to white wines. Sulfites also prevent the growth of yeast or bacteria. Rosé wines have a small amount of tannin structure – which is a natural preservative – that slows down that oxidation and spoilage process, but all wines have sulfites.

To the disappointment of many who feel sulfites are bad for them, there is no such thing as a "sulfite-free" wine. Consumers who are concerned about sulfites can opt for wines that have "low sulfites" or "no added sulfites," most commonly found in natural, organic, sustainable and biodynamically produced wines.

There are some people who can have an adverse reaction to sulfites. Those are people with sulfite allergies, digestive sensitivities or respiratory issues that could be trigged by this element in wine.

Unfortunately, sommeliers, winemakers and wine sales associates cannot determine how your body will react with sulfites if you have any of those conditions. In that sense, it is best to consult a primary doctor, nutritionist, dietician and / or allergist to determine how best to integrate wine into your life.

CHAPTER THREE: **the grapes**

This tiny little thing.

Who would have ever imagined that this one small thing could capture the love, attention and admiration of millions of millions of people for thousands and thousands of years across several different continents!

It's kind of miraculous when you think about it.

When 600 to 800 of these mini pieces of fruit are pressed together, they magically morph into one bottle of wine that wields a massive amount of power over people.

They help inspire prosé and poetry. They help connect people. They help magnify gatherings in such a way that make them sometime silly, sometimes spontaneous, but always special.

And, personally, they make me feel all warm, fuzzy and all wonderful on the inside.

This entity is none other than the wine grape.

When it comes to the production of wines in the pink category, there is no way to make a rosé wine without red-skin grapes.

However, as we learned in CHAPTER TWO: **the styles and structures**, there are a few ways to achieve the pink color: bleeding or blending.

Yet at the center of it all are the red grapes. A winemaker can take nearly any red-skin grape, out of thousands of available options, to produce a rosé.

However, for the sake of the size of this chapter and the number of potential grapes involved in the process, we'll focus on a small cast of grapes.

Before we get into the grapes, let's revisit the term grape varietal / variety first.

Varietal / variety represents the names of specific grapes. Some professionals also refer to them as a grape "variety." However, varietal is how it will be referred to in this book.

In the wine world, the names of varietals come from the Vitis vinifera species of grapes. This Vitis vinifera species is known as the wine grape with origins linked to Mesopotamia – areas that are now modern-day Iran, Iraq, Georgia, North Africa, Armenia, Syria and Turkey.

There are thousands of grape varietals from the vinifera species found globally in the world. Experts have estimated that there are between 5,000 to 10,000 grape varietals from this species that have developed over the last 8,000-plus years.

For the grapes in this chapter, we will focus on 18 of the most used red grapes that make up today's rosé wine from around the world.

As I've done in my previous book, I am going to write about these grapes as if they are people. I find it is interesting to personify the grapes a bit and focus on their unique characters, since much of trying to understand a wine is done by dissecting the grape's characteristics and personality.

Since we will focus on the unique characteristics of these grapes, the grape varietals will be the main "characters" in this chapter.

Like great characters, some of these grapes transform into members of the chorus line. Some will be crucial members of an all-star cast. And some will be stand-alone sensations.

Let's take a closer look at this small cast of red grapes – listed in alphabetical order.

: blaufränkisch

The name of this grape is a bit of a mouthful to pronounce and that same sentiment extends to the palate. If you say it fast, it almost sounds like sneezing. As a red wine, Blaufränkisch **(blahw-frahn-keesh)** is inky in color and full of dark fruit, purple flowers and hints of spice. As a rosé, it is transformed into a pink, onion-skin colored wine with tart red currant, savory spice notes and high acidity. With ties to Austria from the 1700s where most of the plantings in the world exist, it has made its way into the hearts of winemakers in places like Hungary, Oregon, Germany and New York where it is called Lemberger. Typically, Blaufränkisch grows well in cooler climates, but can stand a little bit of heat as it takes its time to ripen.

: cabernet franc

Usually one to take the backseat to its more famous offspring, Cabernet Sauvignon, the Cabernet Franc **(kab-er-nay frahn)** grape makes a lot of memorable appearances as a rosé wine. Cabernet Franc is most closely linked to the Bordeaux region where its blended with the other regional grapes like Cabernet Sauvignon, Merlot, Malbec and Petit Verdot in a classic Bordeaux blend. As a result, it is also one of the primary grapes used to make rosé Bordeaux blends. These rosé wines tend to be medium in color with hints of raspberry, pink grapefruit and fresh minerality. As a single varietal red, it is known for peppery notes along with black currant, tobacco and hints of flowers in Loire Valley, France, but presents more generous fruit in warmer regions around the world. The grape takes center stage when it shows up as a rosé in places like the Loire Valley, Oregon, Sonoma County and New York. These expressions can range from red current and bell pepper with hints of salt and flint in the Loire to strawberry, apple and honeydew melon and a vegetal green freshness in places in the United States.

: cabernet sauvignon

In terms of a red wine, Cabernet Sauvignon **(kab-er-nay soh-vin-yohn)** is known as being "the gold standard:" classic, relevant and timeless. It is, undeniably, one of the most regal, noble and respected red grapes on the planet. But in the rosé world, this grape varietal only makes small, special appearances in certain styles – and mostly blends. As a red wine, it is a true superstar, all over the world it boasts generous black berry, black currant and blue berry jam notes. But as a rosé it only makes appearances in places like Bordeaux, Napa Valley, South Africa, and handful of other stops within new world wine regions. In a Bordeaux blend, it is blended with Merlot, Cabernet Franc, Malbec and Petit Verdot for a medium-bodied, medium pink rosé. Cabernet Sauvignon also makes its way into some Provence rosé wines in small percentages. Some of the most distinctive rosé Cabernet Sauvignon expressions tend to be in South Africa where there is a generous dose of a "gamey" quality blended with cherry and goji berry notes with a richer deeper color. However, there are some productions of White Cabernet Sauvignon in the United States. This is a blush style from California that tends to be a saignée method pink wine featuring deeper colors and some potential residual sugar.

: carignan / mazuelo

Carignan (**karin-yan**) is a very adaptable grape. It can grow and thrive in some of the most challenging climates found in Spain, where it goes by the name Mazuelo (**mah-thweh-loh**), and along the Mediterranean Sea regions of Languedoc-Roussillon, Croatia, Sardinia and Provence to name a few areas. As a red wine it can wear many hats. It adds texture to blends, enhances the color and provides generous dried cranberry, earth and floral notes. Serving as an integral Provençal and Côtes du Rhône rosé, it also adds color and fruit. But on it is own, in places like California, it abounds with fresh watermelon, watermelon rind and crushed seashells.

: cinsault / cinsaut

Cinsault (**san-soh**) is easy to like. It has so many amazing attributes. It's a very engaging grape. It's fresh, fruity and flavorful. It's strong and resistant. When combined with other grapes from the places from the South of France to South Africa, it adds nice softness, aroma and generous pomegranate notes and baking spices. It is well traveled, showing up in places like Lebanon, Morocco, Italy, the U.S., and Algeria. Being the international grape of mystery, it goes by a few names. It is recognized as Cinsaut in some locations and as Hermitage in South Africa. It's a regular part of the South of France rosé blends, along with Carignan, Syrah, Grenache and Mourvèdre. The grape adds some lovely aromatic notes, a light color and savory flavors to its rosé blends.

: grenache noir / garnacha

Grenache noir (**gruh-nahsh nwahr**) is smooth, spicy, seductive and bold. It's a darling in the wine world when making amazing single varietal reds from several prominent wine regions around the world. Interesting enough, this grape is indigenous to Spain where it is called Garnacha (**gahr-nah-chah**). But it has found a happy place when blended with grapes like Syrah, Carignan, Cinsault and Mourvèdre red blends primarily in the Southern Rhône Valley down to the Languedoc-Roussillon and Provence. As a red wine, the grape provides generous fruit, dark-berry flavors and texture. Grenache is also a darling in the rosé world, where it is one of the most ideal grapes to use to produce rosé. As a single varietal rosé or in a blend, it adds vibrant color, spiced cherry and apricot notes, and a silky body. The grape is having a lot of success as a single varietal pink wine in the U.S. and in parts of Spain.

: malbec

Malbec (**mahl-behk**) is one of the most invigorating and exciting things – in terms of wine – to have come out of South America. But most people are stunned to learn that the Malbec grape has deep roots in the South of France. The grape was introduced to Argentina in the mid 1800s by the French. In the specific terroir of Argentina, the Malbec characteristics tend to showcase deep fruit notes like plum, black cherry, black currant and blueberry. In Bordeaux, the Malbec grape is typically blended with the other red grapes from that region (Cabernet Franc, Cabernet Sauvignon, Merlot, Petit Verdot) to make up the classic red blend. The rosé Malbec tends to stand mostly on its own in Argentina and in Cahors, France. Malbec also makes its way into the rosé Bordeaux blends. As a single varietal rosé, the wine tends to be deep cherry or even maroon in color. These styles have moderate acid which makes them smoother on the palate providing it with a richer mouthfeel. These are easy drinking styles that work very well with food that's medium to full in texture. Besides Argentina and France, Malbec is also grown in Chile, Italy, Spain, South Africa, New Zealand and the United States, but in much smaller quantities.

: merlot

Merlot (**mer-loh**) is as beautiful as it is misunderstood. It as elegant as it is strong, and it is as famous as it is ignored. Originally from France, Merlot commands the love and admiration of Right Bank Bordeaux wine lovers and critics alike. As a red wine, a bottle of Merlot can be sold for as little as $5 or can go up to $2,600. The prominent notes include everything from plush plum, mocha and cherry to black cherry, eucalyptus and rhubarb. The versatility of Merlot is extraordinary. It has a lot to offer and has a wide mass appeal. However, as a rosé it doesn't get a lot of room to play and show itself off. It's primarily used in rosé Bordeaux blends, paired with Cabernet Sauvignon, Cabernet Franc, Malbec and Petit Verdot. Those are medium-bodied, medium pink colored rosés. Then there are some productions of White Merlot, a blush wine from California, which tend to be saignée method pink wines with deeper colors and some residual sugar.

: montepulciano

The grape Montepulciano (**mohn-tel-pool-chi-ah-nooh**) from the Abruzzo region of Italy – more commonly referred to as Montepulciano d'Abruzzo – is the ultimate pizza wine. From the eastern coast of Italy off the Adriatic Sea, the Montepulciano grape gets a nice amount of heat to produce a fairly juicy and easy-going wine with ripe cherry notes, spice and a hint of flint minerality. The rosé form is also ideal with pizza. The rosato form is called Cerasuolo d'Abuzzo with the Italian word "cerasuolo" translating to "cherry-red" in English. The wine is a deeper ruby in color, medium bodied with faint hints of orange, dried cranberry and a little spice.

: mourvèdre / monastrell

Despite having such a complex name, the Mourvèdre (**moor-veh-druh**) grape is incredibly down to Earth. There is a Sun-baked Earthly quality – on the nose and on the palate – to this grape that also features notes of violets, black berries, café mocha and herbs. Mourvèdre is another indigenous Spanish grape, known as Monastrell (**maw-nehs-trell**). It is a slow ripening grape that best develops in warmer climates. As a result, it is a favorite planting in California and Australia as part of the GSM blends (Grenache, Syrah, Mourvèdre), various regions in Spain like Jumilla and Alicante, and it is integral to the blends that come out of the southern Rhône Valley, Provence and Languedoc-Roussillon. When blended with Grenache, Syrah, Carignan and Cinsault as a rosé, Mourvèdre contributes red plum, purple flower, charred wood with hints of perfume on the nose.

: petite sirah

Petite Sirah (**peh-teet sih-rah**), also known as Durif (**duh-rif**), is a grape that produces rich, fruit-forward spicy wines with a hint of chocolate covered raisins in its red wine form. The word "petite" refers to the size of the berries. Planted in an array of warm weather regions like California, Israel, Mexico, Australia and France, the red wine develops a firm tannic structure and deep color from the skins. Besides the heat, the tannic structure is also enhanced by the high skin to juice ratio of the grape due to its small size. There are a handful of producers turning this powerful little grape into a rosé in California. As a rosé, the grape can showcase wild raspberry, blood orange, rose petals and chamomile tea. And its appearance is closer to a red wine than a typical rosé when winemakers opt to use the the saignée method.

: pinot noir

The allure of Pinot Noir (**pee-noh nwahr**) is undeniable. From its striking appearance to its distinctive nose and its graceful mouthfeel, Pinot Noir has that certain "*Je ne sais quoi*" (*I don't know what*) quality. Unfortunately, behind the scenes – from grape to glass – the process isn't so lovely. It can be quite stressful for winemakers. Pinot Noir is very finicky and difficult to grow. With all the challenges it presents to winemakers, the grape can be perceived as somewhat of a "Diva." As a red wine, it has affectionately been coined the "Heartbreak Grape." It needs a "just right" climate in order to grow properly to produce world-class wines offering up hints of raspberry, cherry, cranberry, wet leaves, pepper and flinty minerality. But as a rosé, winemakers have a little more control over the grape through the limited maceration process. It converts the grape into distinctive qualities of raspberry, cranberry, underripe cherry and roses with a dash of salt and pepper with vibrant acidity. Pinot Noir is native of Burgundy, France, but can also be grown and produced in the Loire Valley, Argentina, Oregon, Northeastern Italy, Chile and California.

: sangiovese

The Sangiovese (**san-joh-vay-zeh**) grape is very much representative of the phrase "it's complicated." It is a suave and sturdy grape with hints of aristocracy. It does reign supreme in the region of Tuscany from the villages of Chianti over to Montepulciano and then on to Montalcino. Fans of the grape have also planted the grape in Corsica, France, Washington State and California. As a red wine, it ranges from a medium-bodied wine with red cherry, plum skin and cranberry tea notes to a bolder wine with black cherry, herbs, leather and firewood. When produced as a single varietal rosé, it becomes a bright, versatile wine with tart red berries, orange peel and a hint of olive.

: syrah / shiraz

Bold, burly and robust with a brooding appearance, Syrah (**see-rah**) has a massive presence that is often tempered by its lush approachability. It's like a big ole Teddy Bear you want to cuddle up with. Syrah is a supple, spicy red wine that is so dynamic that it regularly goes by two names. As you might have guessed, Syrah is the French name. That name is used for grapes found in various regions of France, Spain, Italy, Greece, North America and South America. Shiraz (**she-raz**) is an Australian take on the name Syrah, also used in South Africa. As a red wine, the grape can range from medium-bodied, herbaceous, spicy, meaty and Earthy to rich, ripe, spicy with generous blackcurrant, ripe plum, campfire and mixed-berry jam. Blends of rosé Syrah abound in the Southern Rhône Valley and other parts in the South of France where the grape is blended with Grenache, Cinsault, Carignan and Mourvèdre. Other regions around the world utilize it in the form of GSM (Grenache, Syrah, Mourvèdre) blends. In rosé form, Syrah provides texture, red plum notes and pink peppercorn.

: tempranillo

Bright, spirited and with loads of personality, the Tempranillo (**tem-pra-nee-yo**) grape is an attention getter. And the attention is well deserved. It produces a medium-bodied red wine with dark berry notes like dark cherry and black currant along with secondary notes of oak, vanilla and dill. It serves as the top red grape throughout Spain. However, it can stand on its own or can be blended with Garnacha and Graciano grapes to make a red Rioja – from young to well-aged options. While most people are familiar with the grape from the region of Rioja, it is highly planted in Ribera del Duero and Navarra in Spain, Portugal, California and Washington State. Pink Tempranillo wines from around the world tend to be medium-bodied, ranging from pale to medium pink in color with melon and dragon fruit notes.

: tibouren

This grape makes the rare appearance from time to time, but in the most popular rosé producing region in the world. Tibouren (**tea-bore-rwen**) is mostly used as a blending grape along with Syrah, Grenache, Carignan, Cinsault and Mourvèdre. It can be challenging to grow in the region due to its tendency to bud early, but some producers have had success showing off its unique woodsy, herbal tea and floral notes. Therefore, they use it as the primary grape in some highly distinctive Provence rosé blends. Some of the largest and oldest Tibouren grape vines can be found along the coasts between Nice and Marseille, but overall plantings are small in the region. Look for this grape variety when you want to geek out by yourself or with some close wine loving friends.

: zinfandel

This grape has a serious case of mistaken identity. Some people think the Zinfandel (**zin-fun-dell**) only makes pink wine. Some people think it is indigenous to California. And some people don't know how to identify it. Besides Cabernet Sauvignon, Zinfandel is probably the red grape most linked to California. That is part of the reason some people think it is from California, when it is really linked to the Primitivo (**pri-meh-tee-voh**) grape originally from Croatia and Puglia, Italy. In all three environments, the grape experiences warm-weather conditions ensuring a well-ripened grape full of juicy dark fruit and spice potential. Another reason this grape is so closely connected to California is due to the popularity and success of the blush wine category that was developed in the 1970s. White Zinfandel is the pink version of the grape. Typically made in the saignée method, it produces a medium-pink color wine that features some residual sugar. However, there are some Zinfandel producers that are making dry rosé versions from the grape using the limited maceration process.

: zweigelt

The Zweigelt (**zvy-gelt**) is like a Frankenstein of the wine world and wow is it alive. Coming into existence as a laboratory grape crossing using the varietals Blaufränkisch and St. Laurent, Dr. Zweigelt created this new red grape varietal in 1922 at the Imperial School of Viticulture and Horticulture in Austria. The doctor created a grape that, as a red wine, has tart red fruit notes with some spice and umami characteristics. It works nicely as a summer red. However, in its rosé form, the acid is racy and the tart wild strawberry notes are accentuated along with a healthy dose of salinity. Mostly planted in other parts of Europe like Hungary and Slovakia, you can also find some distinctive rosé options in the Finger Lakes in New York.

CHAPTER FOUR: **the place**

Whew! Yes! We have arrived at "the place." I can relax a bit!

This is a very important stop on our rosé wine education journey to really understand how wines smell, taste and feel the way they do.

My Virgo mind was feeling a little anxious, if you couldn't tell already, because the sense of place is highly important to me as a sommelier and wine educator.

Normally, I prefer to feature "the place" as chapter two in a book. But I get it. I totally get it.

The lure of what rosé represents makes it easy to get lost in the color, the style, the occasion and the fun of it all.

The "sense of place" tends to take a backseat.

That could be one reason why some wine professionals refuse to see rosé as a valid wine.

That sense of place associated with many pink wines might not radiate from the glass like maybe a white Burgundy or a red Bordeaux. As a result, pink wines are potentially not be considered as interesting or dynamic as those options.

That happens when comparing various wine styles against each other. These are very different things. It's like comparing apples to oranges or pears to peaches. They are just different.

While some of these pink wines might not carry the same type of cache as other wines, the sense of place still connects them to the characteristics, personality and dignity of the land.

There is no getting around that.

Therefore, in this chapter, I want to honor and shine some much-needed light on all the people, places and environmental elements that contribute to the signature regional styles of pink wines from across the globe.

I must warn you, though.

This chapter might be a little more appealing to many of my fellow wine nerds and cork dorks.

Essentially, we are going to be looking at the connections between nature and nurture and then how things turn out as a result of both.

We'll first pull back the curtain on some of the philosophical approaches to handling the vineyard. That revolves around understanding the environment, the connection to the land, and both the traditional and innovative ways of caring for its health and longevity.

That's the nurture part.

Then we will look at the wine world from a top-lined scientific perspective. That is to encourage rosé consumers to get more familiar with how certain styles evolve based on regional attributes.

That's the nature part.

Lastly, we'll pay special attention to some prominent wine regions and the assortment of wines produced within the subregions. We'll connect the dots to how the environment, philosophical approaches and global locations play in role in why you smell what you smell and taste what you taste in a glass of pink wine.

This chapter won't exactly be linear in structure, but it should prove quite interesting.

Oh! And there will be a little more French thrown in for fun.

: the terroir

Each wine region is equipped with its own geographical gifts that are distinct to that small or large section of land. It is a regional character that shines through. It is the wine's natural identity. It is like having the fingerprints of a place all over the wine.

In the wine world, we call that "terroir."

Terroir is a French word that translates into the word "soil" in English. This short word, however, extends so much further than just the soil of a parcel of land. The concept of terroir basically encapsulates the overall environment in which the grapes are grown on the vines.

That includes the soil – the mineral makeup of a piece of land – as well as the climate, the weather, sun exposure, vineyard conditions, proximities to bodies of water, altitude and other variables.

Despite the current effort by some winemakers to create a Provençal style rosé outside of Provence, terroir is what makes the "place" of where a wine comes from so special.

This is very important because a land's unique terroir cannot be replicated or reproduced in any other place outside of that area.

Terroir might be a French term, but it universally speaks to the taste of the place in the glass which is transmitted by the grape varietal or varieties.

Through viticulture – vine agriculture – regional stewards in the form of grape growers and winemakers use the terroir as a way of paying homage to the land. These professionals have a strong relationship with the land, so they respect its history and practices of a wine region.

They nurture it, they listen to it and they become one with it.

To extract the unique terroir, some of these professionals opt to showcase their land by using specific farming practices in their day-to-day management of the land.

There is a renewed interest in taking better care of the land, the vines and the grapes after the various mistakes made during the industrial revolution in the early 1900s. As those mistakes carried on through to the industrial agriculture movement in the 1950s, many of these vineyard managers and winemakers want to do better for the land and the consumers of their products.

That sentiment is honored and practiced with much vigor in several pink wine producing regions, particularly in Provence.

For some, that means only using organic or all-natural means to protect the vineyards from dangerous herbs, pests and fungi. That involves steering clear of any harsh chemicals related to the care of the land. They do not want to damage the unique biodiversity of the soil or cause any erosion.

Others will take it a step further. These farmers utilize a holistic farming approach called biodynamic farming to protect its environment.

In biodynamic viticulture, organic tools are used in the care of the vineyard. However, the maintenance and care are planned and scheduled by the lunar cycle. That takes into consideration the push and pull effects on the Earth from the sun, stars and moon that give life to the land, vines and grapes.

This practice was created in the 1920s by Rudolf Steiner, an Austrian philosopher, scientist and spiritualist. Many farmers outside of the wine space are now practicing biodynamic techniques on many of our agricultural grocery items.

Then there are others who not only want to protect the region's distinct terroir with organic or biodynamic farming practices, they want to ensure that the vineyard is protected and cared for in a way that sets up long-term, sustainable success.

This is the sustainable viticulture perspective.

Sustainability looks at the ecological, economical and socially responsible practices of farming. It takes into consideration energy conservation, packaging, air quality, water quality and transportation emissions. Always growing in scope, practitioners are constantly looking into new, advanced ways to protect the vineyard as well as the overall environment.

These various practices are put in place so the land can produce healthy vines and healthy fruit. Then that fruit can present a strong representation of the vineyard's personality as a pink wine. And those wines are produced to ensure that a significant sense of place comes through on the nose and on the palate.

However, as they take on that labor of love, they contend with environmental issues that are outside of their control.

And some of those conditions can be harsh, which are predetermined by where the regions fall on the planet.

Grape growers and winemakers diligently try to work around them in order to maximize and produce the ideal fruit.

But Mother Nature is the boss.

That leads us to the global wine world.

When taking a broader look at understanding the role on the place in relation to pink wines, it encapsulates a few major themes:
- Climate zones
- Traditional versus modern philosophies
- Overlapping practices

Some of these elements are fixed. Some of them are ever evolving. Some of them are quite fluid.

We'll take a quick, but comprehensive overview of each of the major concepts to present a fuller picture to better understand terroir from a much wider perspective.

: the climate zones

I'm not sure the last time you've seen the Earth from a satellite view from outer space, but the Earth is gorgeous.

But it is very particular as well, as it should be.

There are only so many places that this Blue planet of ours allows wine grapes to grow and develop properly.

From a macro level – as if we were looking down on the Earth or viewing a map – there are ideal sections of the world that produce these grapes.

These specific places fall between the 30th and 50th parallel in latitude in both the Northern and Southern Hemispheres of the world, divided by the Earth's equator.

Let's take the Northern Hemisphere first.

In the case of the Northern Hemisphere, from the top-down perspective – the North Pole toward the Equator – the latitude for grape growing goes from 50 degrees latitude in the north to 30 degrees in the south. Wine regions that populate this half of the winemaking world include Austria, France, Italy, Spain, Germany, Portugal, North America, Canada, North Africa, Eastern Europe, The Middle East, China, Japan and a portion of India.

The 50th degree latitude represents the coldest conditions in which grapes can be properly grown. It gets too cold to suitably grow and cultivate grapes further north of that top range.

The 30th parallel represents the southernmost extremities and warmest areas where these grapes can effectively grow and be turned into wine. Too far below that and it gets too hot to cultivate grapes for winemaking.

Then the wine world flips in the Southern Hemisphere.

In that Hemisphere, the 30th parallel is in the north, closer to the Equator, where temperatures are warmer. That puts the 50th parallel in the south, closer to Antarctica and the South Pole where temperatures are colder.

The grapes like to be comfortable. They enjoy a supportive environment. In these sections of the Earth, the grapes achieve proper growth and maturity throughout the annual growing cycle.

Individual grape varietals have their individual needs.

Some grapes mature better in a cooler climate while other varietals need warmer climates to fully ripen.

These dynamics allow for a certain type of structure to develop in each grape.

Temperature is crucial for that.

That is what makes the 30th to 50th parallels in latitude so significant to our wine regions. This portion of the Earth allows for the temperatures to reach an average annual temperature of between 50- and 68-degrees Fahrenheit.

That is a comfortable and supportive environment for the grapes to do what they need to do.

The temperatures – ranging from cooler climates to warmer climates – are needed to start the flowering of the vines at the beginning of the cycle, the fruit development during the middle of the cycle and the ripening of the grapes through the harvest.

In terms of climate, think more about the long-term weather conditions of a region and not the day-to-day.

Within these various wine regions of the world, grapes grow well in either one of three major climate categories or, at times, they overlap.

CONTINENTAL — This category represents regions that are typically found inland in the wine world. Since these regions tend to be further away from large bodies of water, they can experience less rain and result in drier growing conditions. Also, the temperature can go to extremes over the course of a day and a year. During the day, there can be warm temperatures that can take a drastic drop at night. And looking at the overall year, the summer can be very hot while the winters can be cold enough for ice and snow.

MARITIME — This category represents regions that are typically found much closer to significant bodies of water. The region's closeness to water helps contribute to a steadier, long and even-keeled growing cycle. That leads to warmer summers and cool, but not severely cold winters. Unfortunately, the water can also lead to some potential issues. While the nearby water helps to moderate the region's temperatures, that water can also lead to excessive rain. That can lead to "washed out" flavors in grapes, too much fertility and even mildew. These challenges keep winemakers in these regions on their toes.

MEDITERRANEAN — This category represents regions that are found within the Mediterranean region or exhibit Mediterranean-like characteristics. These areas around the world tend to be warmer than both continental and maritime regions. The growing seasons are long but will exhibit moderate to warm temperatures. Although these regions tend to be near a large body of water, the summers are typically dry, less humid and with a lot of rain occurring in the winter.

: the traditional versus modern philosophies

There are two overarching farming styles, regions, winemaking practices and belief systems: The Old World and The New World.

To help get your head around this faster, think about generational differences you might have with either your parents or your grandparents.

Hopefully there is respect for one another, but both parties don't quite see eye-to-eye on how one chooses to operate.

That is "Old World" and "New World" winemaking in a nutshell.

To elaborate, here is an overview of the two philosophies and practices.

Understanding these concepts can give you tremendous perspective when learning about and breaking down the wine world.

And, yes, this does apply to pink wines.

OLD WORLD – "Old World" is a term that includes geographic regions spanning from the Mediterranean, North Africa, Europe, The Middle East and Asia. That mirrors the wine world as well, with a special emphasis on today's most prominent wine regions in that area like Austria, Italy, France, Germany, Greece, Portugal and Spain.

Winemakers in these regions have been making wines from the vinifera grape species for about 2,000 to 4,000-plus years. Over that time, these professionals had to overcome extreme hurdles: climate change, wars, expanding empires, collapsing empires, challenging landscapes, obsolete technologies, cultural shifts and the ever-evolving wine palate.

It is *the* reason why most Old-World wines are named after the place they come from as opposed to the grape varietal.

Therefore, for Provençal wines, you will see the wine named after the region and not the grape used to make the wine.

That is a way for winemakers to stand apart from other regions, even sometimes within their larger land holdings, and to show the distinct qualities that no other element in the winemaking process can accentuate.

NEW WORLD – New World wine regions, on the other hand, are much different. These are areas spread around the world, outside of the Mediterranean region, that had been inhabited by millions of indigenous people prior to the 1500s.

Unlike the Old World, the New World wine regions are spread out across the world between both hemispheres. In the Northern Hemisphere, the regions include the United States (California, Washington State, New York, Oregon), Canada, China and Japan. Then on the flip side in the Southern Hemisphere, the primary winemaking countries are South America (Chile, Argentina, Brazil, Uruguay), South Africa, Australia and New Zealand.

Though the regions are disconnected physically around the world, they are connected in spirit. That spirit is fiercely attached to innovation, experimentation and the freedom to express the grapes and areas how a winemaker best sees fit. These wine regions do not have to adhere to the same wine laws and regulations found in Old World countries.

: the overlapping practices

This is when it gets tricky.

It also connects to some of the points I was making in the first two chapters.

Many of the pink wines around the world today are being made to fit into one signature style to supply a customer demand.

That happens a lot in the wine world, so it is not a new phenomenon.

The wine world has encountered this problem for some time with wine regions from around the world anxious to produce the next big wine to compete with France: a Bordeaux-style blend or a Champagne-like domestic sparkling wine or a Meursault-style Chardonnay.

With increased global competition there is a mission to create a similar product with mass appeal that captures sales in the category, helping the business stay afloat or potentially cornering a market.

When that happens, it can prove difficult to tell the difference between the two wine worlds when tasted side-by-side.

With the globalization of wine these days, similar traits in climate, winemaking styles, techniques and other factors can allow both styles to bleed into each other.

That is why terroir is so important. It makes a wine distinctive and it cannot be duplicated, no matter how similar a wine tastes to its main competitor.

Getting to know and understand the unique differences between the two worlds can allow you to clearly pick out a Provençal rosé from Bandol apart from a Washington State rosé wine in a blind tasting exercise.

The two wines could be similar, but not the same.

There will always be something very distinctive about the sense of place in each glass. Still, the characteristics of the wine can be similar enough to blur the lines between the two world's styles.

Now, all that information over the last few pages, has culminated to this point.

This is a chance to take what you have learned about the sense of place and drill it down even further.

Well, at least for everyone who is still with me in this chapter and have not decided to skip ahead.

The next section will showcase attributes from four of the largest pink-wine producing countries, along with distinct subregions, to get more familiar with the regional traits, the grapes, the climates and types of wines produced in those regions.

This is also an effort to highlight the diverse regions making the world's rosé wine and hopefully inspire further exploration into the category.

: the prominent rosé regions

Provence seems to have a monopoly on rosé wines.

That has been demonstrated by consumer mindsets and consumer spending as previously outlined in this book.

And, once again, there is absolutely nothing wrong with Provence wines.

It is just that there are a lot of other prominent – and not so prominent – wine regions that are making distinctive and dynamic rosé wine options these days.

A variety of options can create some additional excitement to pink wine consumption worldwide.

With the goal of not overwhelming you with too many details, I utilized a "less is more" approach to present brief facts on these major rosé producing regions to conjure up a greater understanding of these places.

And who better to start with than France, arguably the most recognizable wine producing region in the world.

: France

It is reported that the region of Provence experiences nearly 3,000 hours of sunlight per year. Well, apparently, it seems the sun loves all of France. It has been shining brightly over many of France's winemaking regions. The country represents some of the most sought-after sparkling wines from Champagne, red wines from Burgundy and Bordeaux and now rosé wine from Provence. While the bulk of rosé wines do come from Provence, there are a lot of interesting areas that produce their own pink wines styles from different grapes, in a different terroir and with different philosophies.

Pink wine regions are plentiful in France. In the North, there is the Champagne region that makes amazing rosé bubbles with the use of Pinot Noir and Meunier. There is also a small region in Burgundy that makes still rosé with Pinot Noir. When we get to Loire, we start to see a few more Pinot Noir rosé options out of Sancerre. But then there are slightly fuller – and sometimes faintly sweet – types using Cabernet Franc, Cabernet Sauvignon and Grolleau hailing from other regions of Loire. And we can't forget about the spectrum of Bordeaux red grapes that produce distinctively dry Bordeaux rosé wines.

As we get into the South of France, the colors become a bit richer in Côtes du Rhône and even a deeper pink in regions like Tavel in the southern Rhône Valley using a combination of the Syrah, Grenache, Carignan, Cinsault and Mourvèdre grapes.

Provence is, of course, well known for producing a range of pale, light, dry, crisp rosé wines. But the wines styles can vary from producer to producer. Some have a little more spice. Some have a little more texture. Then, within Provence, there is the Bandol region that has legal grape requirements for its rosé wine production. The blend must contain 50 percent of Mourvèdre, which is the preferred red grape in Bandol, along with Grenache, Cinsault with restricted amounts of Syrah and Carignan allowed. The Bandol rosé wines are rich, elegant, Earthy and can be consumed with some age.

Lastly, off the beaten path, a lovely surprise in the form of rosé pops up on the French Island of Corsica. This is the birthplace of Napoleon Bonaparte and gets its winemaking roots from the Italians. A small amount of rosé made from the Nielluccio grape is produced, which is known as Sangiovese in Italy.

Below is a simple snapshot of these regions, from the northern regions to the southern regions. Any white grapes used in the region will be placed within parentheses.

CHAMPAGNE ROSÉ
Major regions: Montagne de Reims, Vallée de la Marne, Côte des Blancs, Côte de Sezanne, Aube
Styles: Sparkling rosé – Non-vintage, Vintage
Grapes: Pinot Noir, Meunier, (Chardonnay)
Dryness level: Brut Nature/Brut Zero, Extra Brut, Brut, Demi-sec, Doux
Soil: Chalk, clay, silt
Climate: Maritime, Continental
Latitude: 48.9 degrees; Northern Hemisphere

BURGUNDY ROSÉ
Major regions: Chablis, Marsannay, Mercurey
Styles: Still rosé and sparkling rosé: Cremant
Grapes: Pinot Noir, Gamay, (Chardonnay)
Soil: Limestone
Weather: Continental
Latitude: 47 to 46.9 degrees; Northern Hemisphere

LOIRE VALLEY ROSÉ
Major regions: Chinon, Touraine, Anjou
Styles: Still rosé and sparkling rosé: Cremant
Grapes: Cabernet Franc, Gamay, Cabernet Sauvignon, Pinot Noir, Grolleau, (Chardonnay), (Chenin Blanc), (Sauvignon Blanc)
Soil: Gravel, slate, sandstone, schist, volcanic rock, flint, limestone
Weather: Maritime
Latitude: 47.5 degrees; Northern Hemisphere

RHÔNE VALLEY ROSÉ
Major regions: Tavel, Gigondas, Vacqueyras, Côtes du Rhône
Styles: Still rosé

Grapes: Carignan, Grenache, Cinsault, Syrah, Mourvèdre
Soil: Limestone, slate, sand
Weather: Mediterranean, Alpine
Latitude: 45.7 degrees; Northern Hemisphere

BORDEAUX ROSÉ

Major regions: Various locations throughout Bordeaux
Styles: Still rosé and sparkling rosé: Cremant
Grapes: Cabernet Sauvignon, Cabernet Franc, Carménère,
Merlot, Malbec, Petit Verdot
Soil: Clay, limestone, gravel, sand
Climate: Maritime
Latitude: 44.8 degrees; Northern Hemisphere

PROVENCE ROSÉ

Major regions: Côtes de Provence, Coteaux d'Aix-en-Provence,
Coteaux Varois en Provence, Bandol
Styles: Still rosé and sparkling rosé
Grapes: Carignan, Cinsault, Syrah, Grenache, Mourvèdre,
Merlot, Cabernet Sauvignon, Tibouren, (Rolle)
Soil: Limestone, Volcanic
Climate: Mediterranean, Alpine
Latitude: 44 degrees; Northern Hemisphere

LANGUEDOC-ROUSSILLON ROSÉ

Major regions: Minervois, La Clape, Pic Saint-Loup, Cabrieres
Styles: still rosé and sparkling rosé: Cremant
Grapes: Carignan, Cinsault, Syrah, Grenache, Mourvèdre,
Merlot, Cabernet Sauvignon
Soil: Limestone, sandstone, schists, calcareous-clay, sand, silt
Weather: Mediterranean, semi-Continental
Latitude: 43.5 degrees; Northern Hemisphere

CORSICA ROSÉ

Major regions: Patrimonio, Ajaccio
Styles: Still rosé
grapes: Nielluccio, Sciacarello, Grenache
Soil: Chalk, clay
Weather: Mediterranean
Latitude: 42 degrees; Northern Hemisphere

: Spain

As the world's third largest producer of pink wine, Spain can go from producing lush, inexpensive deep pink rosados in different parts of the country to luxury Gran Reserva rosado options from Rioja. Navarra and Rioja are two well-known places where rosado has been produced primarily utilizing the Tempranillo and Garnacha grapes. In Rioja, one of the other main red grapes, Graciano, can be found as either part of the rosado blend or as a single varietal pink wine.

In Navarra – in which rosado accounts for nearly half of its wine production – winemakers might add a little Cabernet Sauvignon and Merlot into the mix as well. The region also likes to experiment with a few different winemaking techniques like a six to 12-hour maceration time, the saignée method (sangrado in Spanish), barrel aging and sur-lie production where the yeast is left with the juice to produce a distinctive taste and richer mouthfeel.

Sparkling wine out of Spain – in the form of Cava – can be amazing in its pink form. Blending red Spanish grapes from Penedès in with the traditional white grape base can yield a variety of results, ranging from salty strawberry and hibiscus to soft cherry, bitter orange and rhubarb notes.

Below is a simple snapshot of these regions, from the northern regions to the southern regions. Any white grapes used in the regions will be placed within parentheses.

BASQUE COUNTRY ROSADO
Major regions: Getariako Txakolina, Bizkaiko Txakolina and Arabako Txakolina
Styles: Still rosado wines with slight effervescence
Grapes: Hondarrabi Beltza, (Hondarribi Zuri) and (Hondarrabi Zuri Zerratia)
Soil: Sandy, loose alluvial, clay, limestone
Weather: Maritime
Latitude: 42.9 degrees; Northern Hemisphere

RIOJA ROSADO
Major regions: Rioja Alta, Rioja Oriental and Rioja Alavesa
Styles: Still rosado wines
Grapes: Tempranillo, Garnacha, Graciano, Mazuelo, Maturana tinta (Viura)
Soil: Alluvial, ferruginous clay, calcareous clay
Weather: Continental, Mediterranean
Latitude: 42.7- 42.3 degrees; Northern Hemisphere

NAVARRA ROSADO
Major regions: Baja Montaña, Valdizarbe and Tierra de Estella
Styles: Still rosado wines
Grapes: Cabernet Sauvignon, Garnacha, Graciano, Mazuelo, Merlot, Tempranillo, Syrah
Soil: Sand, marl, loam, limestone, gravel
Weather: Continental with Maritime influences
Latitude: 42.7 degrees; Northern Hemisphere

LA MANCHA ROSADO
Major regions: Castilla-La Mancha
Styles: Still, sparkling rosado wines
Grapes: Tempranillo
Soil: Limestone, chalk, red clay
Weather: Continental
Latitude: 41.83 degrees; Northern Hemisphere

PENEDES ROSADO
Major regions: Alt Penedès, Penedès Central, Baix Penedès
Styles: Still, sparkling rosado wines
Grapes: Monastrell, Mazuelo, Trapat, Merlot, Cabernet
Sauvignon, Sumoll, (Macabeo), (Xarel-lo), (Parellada)
Soil: Sandy, clay, cretaceous limestone
Weather: Continental and Maritime
Latitude: 41.4 degrees; Northern Hemisphere

: Italy

Italy is one of the world's most classic wine regions. And, for a
long time, it had a robust production of the Italian pink wine called
rosato. However, as other countries like France and the U.S.
increased their production, it seemed that Italy decreased its
production and local consumption. Research shows that from 2002
to 2018, production of rosato wine had decreased significantly. In
2002, Italy produced 21 percent of the world's pink wine. But, by
2018, the country only accounted for 9 percent of pink wine
production.

With the rosé boom, there is an ever-increasing number of Italian
winemakers producing some remarkable pink wine. In the northern
region of Veneto, the region has made rosato still and sparkling
wine using a combination of grapes like Corvino, Rondinella and
Pinot Nero. The signature style is called Chiaretto di Bardolino.
The sparkling wines were referred to as spumante rosato (sparkling
pink) wines, even if they were made like a Prosecco using the
Charmat method. It was illegal for any sparkling wine to be named
a Prosecco that wasn't made from 100 percent of the Glera grape.
Now, the government-controlled designation of origin (DOC)
Consortium in Veneto has allowed the addition of the Pinot Nero
grape to be added to Glera to make a Prosecco rosato. Bottles
should start hitting the market in 2021 with the new designation.

Moving down and west to the Tuscany region, the Sangiovese
grape has made a nice splash locally and across the world with its

bright yet earthy notes. Further down and to the south-central part of Italy along the Adriatic Sea the bright, cherry red Cerasulo d'Abuzzo has become legendary in some circles.

All the way down to the southern island of Sicily, the winemakers continue to push the winemaking envelope with their homegrown grape varietals, sometimes mixed with international varietals, to producing one-of-a-kind, Earth-driven rosato wines in high elevations areas near Mt. Edna.

Below is a simple snapshot of these regions, from the northern regions to the southern regions. Any white grapes used in the regions will be placed within parentheses.

VENETO ROSATO
Major regions: Bardolino, Valdobbiadene
Styles: Still, sparkling rosato wine
Grapes: Corvina, Rondinella, Pinot Nero, (Glera)
Soil: Volcanic, clay, calcareous
Weather: Continental, Maritime
Latitude: 45.44 degrees; Northern Hemisphere

TUSCANY ROSATO
Major regions: Bolgheri, Terre di Pisa,
Styles: Still rosato wine
Grapes: Sangiovese, Cabernet Sauvignon, Merlot, Syrah
Soil: Clay, sand, limestone, sandstone
Weather: Mediterranean
Latitude: 43.77 degrees; Northern Hemisphere

ABRUZZO ROSATO
Major regions: Abruzzo
Styles: Still rosato wine
Grapes: Montepulciano
Soil: Calcareous clay, sand
Weather: Mediterranean
Latitude: 42.19 degrees; Northern Hemisphere

SICILY ROSATO
Major regions: Mount Etna
Styles: Still rosato wine
Grapes: Nerello Mascalese, Nero d'Avola, Syrah
Soil: Volcanic, limestone, clay, silt, rocky
Weather: Mediterranean
Latitude: 37.60 degrees; Northern Hemisphere

: United States of America

The U.S. might forever go down in wine history as the country that created blush wine with its flagship product in the category being White Zinfandel. It was that American ingenuity that turned a minor problem into a major profit. White Zinfandel has gone on to sale an average of 3 million cases every year for several decades. This type of wine, within the pink wine category, is just one side of the rosé wine story in the U.S. Around the same time blush wine was being created, America was also being recognized as a major force to be reckoned with in the wine industry. These wines from the States were not only on par with French wines, in some cases, they surpassed them.

Transitioning from the perception of a country full of bulk, jug wines to wines of high quality and structure, the rosé wine production eventually moved into more dry styles that were like what you might find in France, Italy and Spain. Grenache, Pinot Noir, Cabernet Franc and Gamay were some of the grapes used to make these dry rosé wine in various parts of California, Washington State, Oregon and New York State.

The post-Phyloxera love affair with French grape varietals in the U.S. also allowed for the "South of France" blends to be produced, with Mourvèdre and Syrah being used. Rosé sparkling wines, also inspired by the French Champagne styles, were being produced with Chardonnay and doses of Pinot Noir and Meunier.

While California produces about 90 percent of all the wine in the U.S., New York rosé wines have developed quite the following. Wölffer Estate, a wine producer in the Hamptons, using a mixture of red and white grape varietals blended together. The vineyard's popularity continued to grow with its sequential releases of other rosés like "Summer in a Bottle," rosé cider and a rosé made from land the company owns in Mendoza, Argentina.

The demand for rosé was so high the summer of 2014 in the Hamptons that it made the national news. The *New York Post* newspaper reported a "rosé shortage" right before the Labor Day holiday. The story was picked up by news outlets around the country.

In the Finger Lakes in Upstate New York, there are several highly distinctive pink wines produced from a variety of grapes. Winemakers in this region use native Vitis labrusca grapes, Vitis vinifera grapes and hybrid grapes to produce a variety of wine styles. Those grape species options are available in many of the smaller wine making regions across the U.S., from Pennsylvania and Virginia to North Carolina and Kansas.

The Pacific Northwest is also showcasing amazing rosé blends inspired by the Southern Rhone Valley in France produced in Washington State and lovely Pinot Noir options inspired by Burgundy, France, from Oregon.

Below is a simple snapshot of a few of these regions, from the northern regions to the southern regions. Any white grapes used in the regions will be placed within parentheses.

WASHINGTON STATE ROSÉ
Major regions: Columbia Valley, Wala Wala Valley
Styles: Still, sparkling rosé wines
Grapes: Cabernet Sauvignon, Cabernet Franc, Grenache, Merlot, Mourvèdre, Syrah, Sangiovese, Tempranillo, (Chardonnay)
Soil: Sandy loam, alluvial, volcanic, silt, basalt
Weather: Maritime, Continental
Latitude: 46.06 degrees; Northern Hemisphere

OREGON ROSÉ
Major regions: Willamette Valley, Chehalem Mountains, Dundee Hills
Styles: Still, sparkling rosé wines
Grapes: Pinot Noir, Meunier (Chardonnay)
Soil: loam, silt, basalt, volcanic
Weather: Maritime, Continental
Latitude: 44.94 degrees; Northern Hemisphere

NEW YORK ROSÉ
Major regions: Long Island, Finger Lakes, Hudson Valley
Styles: Still, sparkling rosé wines
Grapes: Cabernet Sauvignon, Cabernet Franc, Pinot Noir, Meunier, Merlot, Syrah, Catawba, Saperavi (Chardonnay, Pinot Gris, Pinot Blanc, Riesling, Sauvignon Blanc, Gewurztraminer)
Soil: Gravel, shale, clay, sand
Weather: Maritime, Continental
Latitude: 42.72 to 41.92 degrees; Northern Hemisphere

CALIFORNIA ROSÉ
Major regions: North Coast, Sonoma county, Napa Valley, Central Coast
Styles: Still rosé and blush wines; sparkling rosé
Grapes: Cabernet Sauvignon, Cabernet Franc, Cinsault, Merlot, Mourvèdre, Pinot Noir, Grenache, Sangiovese, Syrah, Zinfandel, Petite Sirah, (Chardonnay)
Soil: Sand, loam, clay, volcanic ash, silt
Weather: Maritime, Mediterranean
Latitude: 38.29 to 30.84 degrees; Northern Hemisphere

: the additional regional considerations

We only got to focus on a fraction of the rosé wine producing world, looking at some of the biggest producers. There is, however, a mix of Old World and New World, Northern Hemisphere and Southern Hemisphere regions to also take into consideration.

<u>Old World / Northern Hemisphere</u>: Austria and Portugal

If we look at two Old World winemaking countries that also happen to both fall in the Northern Hemisphere, we find two vastly different countries producing highly distinctive pink wine.

First up, we have Austria. Wine has been made in this region for about 4,000 years, pre-dating the occupancy of the Roman Empire. It is a country mostly known for its white grape varietals, but the region can also successfully produce red grape varietals that thrive in cooler weather conditions like Blaufränkisch, Pinot Noir and Zweigelt. When these grapes are turned into rosé wine, they offer vibrant, tangy and mineral driven wines that can compete with rosé styles found throughout the Loire Valley of France or Italian rosatos from Lombardy and Veneto.

Next we have Portugal, a country best known for its decadent sweet Port, Madeira and hearty red wines. However, in regions like the Douro, Alentejo and Vinho Verde, there are some diverse pink wine options being produced. Being nestled in between the Atlantic Ocean and Spain, Portugal has varied climate regions suitable for a slew of grape varietals for rosé or rosado production like Vinhão, Rabo de Anho, Touriga Nacional, Moreto, Padeiro, Espareido, Rabo-de-Anho. Therefore, you can choose from the light, slightly fizzy pink Vinho Verde wines or more textured styles from the Douro or Alentejo.

New World / Southern Hemisphere: South Africa and Argentina

If we turn our attentions over to New World countries that both fall in the Southern Hemisphere of the world, we have two countries that are making some big, bold rosé wines.

We will look at South Africa first. South Africa has been increasing its production and consumption of rosé steadily for a 10-year period. In 2018, the country was the fifth largest producer of rosé wine, coming in after Italy. In terms of red grapes, the country is fond of grape varietals from French regions like Bordeaux and the southern Rhône Valley. Therefore, rosé options that primarily feature Cabernet Sauvignon or Grenache and Syrah blends are a lot creamier and smoother than most rosé wines on the market.

The same can be said of most of the rosé wines that come out of South America. In Argentina, rosé wines have been known to be made from either Malbec or Pinot Noir. The Malbec rosés have been medium bodied in texture and primarily deeper in color, although more limited maceration options are hitting shelves these days to produce light-bodied options. However, as a New World wine producing country, winemakers have more room to experiment and are combining Pinot Noir and Malbec into a new style of rosé blend in the country.

CHAPTER FIVE: **the personal palate**

It is time to get a little personal.

Up until this point, we've gone over a lot of detail in this book. Hopefully, you are getting a solid understanding of the pink wine category.

But now I want to focus on you.

At the beginning of book, I shared some of my earlier life experiences with pink wines.

For a while, I unintentionally pushed rosé wine out of my life. It wasn't because I wanted to. It just sort of happened as I focused on other styles of wine, hoping to expand my personal palate.

Pink wine didn't seem to fit into the life of the person I was trying to be in the world: educated, sophisticated, successful, cosmopolitan.

I allowed judgement, shame and insecurity to keep me away from wine style that I really enjoyed. It eventually just fell off my radar. I only really got back into rosé when it was deemed "socially acceptable" about 15 years ago.

I have a lot of years of drinking under my belt, if you couldn't already tell.

The thing that saddens me is that I know I am not alone. I know there are some of you reading this chapter that have had similar experiences with wine.

It might not have been with rosé, like in my case.

Maybe it was with a buttery Chardonnay? Maybe it was Riesling? Maybe it was Merlot? Maybe it was value brand? Maybe it was a regional preference?

But at some point, in your life, you were wine shamed.

That's not right. That's not cool. That's not acceptable.

No judgement!
No shame!
No insecurity!

There are a lot of persnickety wine drinkers out there. By all means, people are entitled to their opinions. Lord knows that I have mine.

While we cannot change the behaviors, beliefs or rhetoric of some individuals who appoint themselves as the authorities on proper wine consumption, we can evoke our own power.

That is the power of our personal palates.

The opinions of others don't have to order your steps in terms of your wine consumption.

You decide for yourself.

Wine is for everyone and there is a wine for every single palate type out there in the world.

You, and only you, will truly understand your palate. Be confident and secure in what it likes and focus on the enjoyment of those things. Enjoy what you like – not what someone says you should like.

If you enjoy your rosé with a glass full of ice, enjoy it. If you keep getting judgmental looks because you love a deep, dark pink rosé, ignore them.

If all you ever want to drink in terms of pink is a light, pale, crisp, dry Provence rosé, then do that. If you have rosé sparkling wine with nearly every meal, please invite me over. I think that is super cool. But, again, it is not about me. It's about you.

Own your personal palate.

And to the men!

There is a slew of great, fun, adventurous and gregarious men around the world who really love wine, but some might have some personal reservations about drinking rosé.

Drinking pink wine has nothing to do with gender or "acceptable" gender roles. It is wine. It's not going somehow change the molecular structure of your DNA. Wine can be magical, but it's not quite that powerful.

The only thing you should worry about is if you enjoy it.

If you don't like it, you just don't like it.

Life is too short to drink wine you don't like. But please don't let the color deter you.

If you are not sure if you will like it, the only way to know for sure is to try it. And if you try it and are not sure how you feel about it, that's perfectly fine too. Sometimes a wine will grow on us or it will eventually fall out of our consciousness.

That's perfectly fine and natural.

There is this powerful personal palate paradox when it comes to all wine.

Sometimes there seems to be no rhyme or reason why you like what you like. Then there are those times when you know what you like without the shadow of a doubt.

You don't have to know all the time. There is a type of magic that happens in the not knowing.

That's why wine classes, wine books, wine videos, wine stores and wine bars exist. They are there to help you explore and get lost in the possibilities.

Wine is meant to be enjoyed. It is not something to be ridiculed about.

From this point on, please try not to fall victim to judgment, shame and insecurity regarding your wine choices.

Get a little weird with your rosé choices. Go for something a little obscure. Explore the fringe. Go against the grain.

Many great things happen can inside a person's wheelhouse, but also outside of one's comfort zone.

Cheers to owning what intrinsically belongs to you: your palate, your choices, your life, your time and your interest in pink wine.

CHAPTER SIX: **the food and wine pairings**

This is going to be juicy.

I'm getting hungry just thinking about this chapter.

You might want to consider getting your hands on a little snack as you peruse these pages.

And don't forget your wine.

The conversation about food and wine pairings pops up in nearly every wine class I teach. That is regardless of the topic. It is something that people are genuinely interested in, learning how to maximize their enjoyment of wine and how to pair properly.

When certain food suggestions fall out of my mouth that are often more succulent, decadent and opulent than the cheese, antipasti and crackers in front of the students, there is a collective wave of moans and groans in the form of cravings.

Therefore, securing your favorite snack, meal or cheese board selections, would be wise as we go through some food wine rosé wine pairings.

By this point, you all know that I love wine. I very much enjoy being a sommelier, wine educator and consumer of wines from around the world.

I also love food. I love it so much – not just for fuel, but for enjoyment – that I sometimes joke that I might finally enroll in culinary school in my mid-sixties when my other friends are retiring.

Therefore, pairing wine with food is one of my favorite activities – in both life and in work.

When I learned that a fair share of rosé lovers are not in the regular practice of pairing their pink wines with food, I was rather surprised.

I suppose it goes to back to that concept of enjoying rosé by the beach, pool and parties. People might graze on some cheese, olives and bites of charcuterie, but that's probably the extent of those food and wine interactions.

Well, I'm here to tell you that you can have your rosé wine and successfully pair it with your snacks, soups, salads, entrée and deserts too.

Since pink wines are real wines, just like red and white, the same general food and wine pairing principles apply.

Those principles, unfortunately, can really throw people for a loop given what we've been accustomed to as proper food and wine guidelines: pairing white wine with white meats and red wine with red meats.

If that theory is true, where does that leave pink wines? With pink foods?

Ugh, so sorry for that. I just got a little queasy at the thought of the potential options. If you had a visceral reaction to the thought of pairing pink wine with pink-colored dishes, then you can see that the logic of pairing wine by its color might not be the best approach.

In this chapter, we'll first focus on some "Wine and Food Pairings: 101" considerations. Then we'll see what sticks when these considerations are thrown against some common and uncommon food and wine pairing scenarios.

: the food for thought pairing guidelines

Let's continue with the concept of pairing food and wine by its color.

I know that has been a very common practice around the world from restaurants to homes. And I think that *can* be a good thing at times. It provides a safe guideline to follow for red and white wines.

However, rather than focus on color with color, let's move the conversation over to pairing primarily by the body of the wine with the body of the food.

In terms of body, there are three major body styles when it comes to wines (rosé, red, white, orange). That includes light textures, medium textures and full textures. We covered this in CHAPTER TWO: **the styles and structures**, but it also applies here.

Here is a brief recap:

- Light-bodied wine closely resemble the texture of skim milk; light with a thin coating on your tongue and palate

- Medium-bodied wines are closer in texture to 1 or 2 percent milk or even vegan milk options like rice, almond, oat and soy

- Full-bodied wines have a richer feel like whole milk or half-and-half for my coffee drinkers; however, not as rich as heavy cream

In that sense, pairing now becomes more about matching textures and balancing flavors – regardless of the color of the wine.

Ultimately what we are looking for is balance. Food and wine pairings are put together in the pursuit of balance.

You don't want the wine to overpower the food and you don't want the food to overpower the wine. You want to create a nice, harmonious balance.

You just don't want the items to conflict with each other. Therefore, you would not want to serve a very light rosé with barbecue ribs. The flavor, fat, protein and sauce would severely overpower the wine. But that rosé wine would work well with a lighter dish like soupe de poisson (fish soup) or Shrimp Caesar Salad.

It's like magic. The alchemical balance is spot on and the overall experience can be otherworldly.

> **match body with body**
> not color with color

That is when it is done right.

The wine enhances the food. The food brings out more in the wine. The two balance each other out. And the overall experience is elevated by the pairing.

On the other hand, it can also be gag reflex inducing when it goes oh so wrong.

Am I right or am I right?

To help make your food and wine pairing adventures more successful, here are some rule of thumb considerations.

: the embracing of acid

Pink wines are extremely versatile.

That means that the components of the rosé – alcohol, acidity, flavors and the small amount of tannins – fit with a wide range of dishes.

And in terms of food and wine pairings, the acid content is extremely helpful. Remember, all wines have acid. We learned about acid in CHAPTER TWO: **the styles and structures**.

Rosés tend to have moderate-plus acid to high-acid levels, depending on the climates where the grapes are grown, which we learned in CHAPTER FOUR: **the place**. And sparkling rosé wines boast a higher acid content based on how they are produced.

A little repetition is good for learning and connecting the dots.

Therefore, moderate-plus to high-acid wines are food-loving wines. Acid is an amazing palate-cleanser. It washes your mouth clean of buttery, spicy or meaty flavors, leaving you ready for that next bite.

That's great news in terms of food and wine pairings. Still and sparkling pink wines both work well with a variety of dishes and food styles.

That's a positive attribute that can help limit the risk of a not-so-ideal situation.

But if you find yourself with a serious food and wine pairing dilemma, just remember this: "when in doubt, go the sparkling wine route."

: the pairing approaches

We've covered off on balance, structures, embracing acid and other theories concerning the pairings.

Now let's get into the practical applications.

There are some crucial ways that we can strike a happy balance, allow the food and wine to enhance each other, and have more success in our pairing endeavors.

Remember we are looking for a nice, harmonious balance. To achieve that, we want to use these three philosophies:

1) Pair by complement
2) Pair by contrast
3) Pair with regional foods / cuisines

: the pairing by complement

This type of pairing takes into consideration similarities in both the food and wine. Then the goal is to complement the flavors in both items. You are looking for the ideal companion that will help strengthen the already desirable attributes. Light with light. Heavy with heavy.

PROVENCE ROSÉ + WATERMELON, FETA, PESTO SALAD

For example, let's start with a light, pale, dry, crisp Provence rosé. The wine will have some lovely hints of peach, melon, melon rind, salinity, fresh acid and moderate alcohol. An ideal pairing for that wine could be a Watermelon Salad with feta cheese and pesto. The wine and salad will nicely complement each other. Additional food options could include mussels with white wine sauce, fresh goat's milk cheese or potato chips.

CABERNET SAUVIGNON ROSÉ + SALMON

A more full-bodied rosé, like a Cabernet Sauvignon rosé from South Africa, would need a dish that can stand up against the weight and elevated alcohol content. The wine will have some soft, ripe fruit notes along with baked clay attributes and a hint of tannins. An ideal pairing for this wine would be wild salmon with steamed or sautéed asparagus. Other food items could include pork tacos, mac and cheese and a hamburger.

: the pairing by contrast

This pairing pulls a little bit more from the concept of balance. In this situation, we are looking at food and wine on the opposite spectrum from each other in some form or fashion. When paired together, they mellow or cancel out some of the powerful, harsh or prominent flavors and components.

WHITE ZINFANDEL + SPICY THAI BASIL NOODLES

Let's start with food this time. You have a spicy Thai basil noodles with shrimp. There will be some salty elements, some very spicy peppers and some savory notes coming from the fish and soy sauces. For a dish that will bring some heat onto our palate in the form of spice, you will want to opt for a rosé that will have some residual sugar or one that is more semi-sweet. An ideal rosé to pair with this dish would either be a White Zinfandel or a Rosé d'Anjou. The extra sugar in the wine will tone down the spicy heat of the dish, giving your palate a little cooling relief. The match also culminates into a lovely sweet and savory combination. The wine options can also pair well with Buffalo chicken wings, spicy fish cakes and spicy sushi.

ROSÉ SPARKLING + FRIED CHICKEN

Instead of something spicy, let's opt for a dish that has a healthy amount of salt like Fried Chicken. The chicken has the breading with a variety of spices and is typically finished with a little extra salt after it is removed from the cooking oil. An ideal pairing for this dish would be a sparkling rosé: Champagne, Cava, Prosecco. The sparkling wine will offer some much-needed acid to temper the fat and salt in the dish and the faint red fruits can play nicely with the herbs and spices found in the breading. The sparkling wine options would also pair nicely with Truffle fries with Parmesan and parsley, fried calamari and pork fried rice.

See what I mean? Are you hungry yet?

: the regional pairings

This is a food and wine pairing concept that is tied to the concept of terroir, the sense of place. It stems from the idea that "what grows together, goes together." The belief is that wines are best suited to pair with the dishes that come from the same area. That area can be drilled down to a very specific region within a country or it can be tied to an overall region. For example, it could be Tuscan-specific wines with ingredients from Tuscany or it can be general Italian wines with a variety of traditional Italian meals.

Since this concept is regional based, it can also include one of the other previous pairing practices, complement or contrast, to achieve the ideal pairing.

Coinciding with the top rosé producing regions that were featured in CHAPTER FOUR: **the place**, here are some "what grows together, goes together" considerations.

PROVENCE, France – Cotes de Provence rosé with seafood stew featuring lots of tomatoes, garlic and saffron. The bright acid and mild fruit notes are great ways to balance the bold flavor combinations.

RIOJA, Spain – Rioja Rosado with lamb chops. One of the major dishes consumed throughout Rioja, lamb chops, would make for a delicious match with a smooth Garnacha-based pink Rioja.

ABRUZZO, Italy – Cerasuolo d'Abruzzo with Bruschetta. The cherry red rosato wine makes an excellent complement to the bread topped with mozzarella, salt, oil, tomato and sometimes a little cured meat.

WASHINGTON STATE, United States – Rosé blend with Dungeness Crab. The Dungeness Crab from the Pacific Northwest coast of Washington is a lovely match for a Grenache and Mourvèdre rosé blend.

As you can see, there are a lot of ways to think about pairing your rosé with food. It's not mandatory, of course. It's an individual choice how you want to enjoy your rosé.

: the pink wines in the fall and wintertime

Contrary to popular belief, rosé wine is not just for the warm weather months.

I know. I know. Some of my sommelier friends will disagree. Some of my wine students will question my sanity. Some people reading this book will outright reject that notion.

But you'll see. Just wait.

Remember that pink wines have varied colors, textures and flavors. In terms of pairing, we have evolved from pairing wine by its color. Pairing is done by the body of the wine and the body of the food.

When the cooler temperatures move back in during the fall and winter months, there will be a strong desire for richer, heartier dishes. That is the ideal time to pull out some of those richer, smoother rosé wines – as well as the pink bubbly wine.

These wines are ideal for fall and winter favorites like roasted kabocha squash salad, mac and cheese, duck prosciutto, roasted chicken, beef tartare, turkey, ham and velvety soups.

I just love that there are so many different options to think about.

Ultimately the goal of this chapter is to encourage you to have fun with both your food and your wine. Experiment with the pairings! Take some risks! Get lost in the process!

Sometimes the best way to learn is by learning what does not work. And that is far too easy for anyone to make happen!

CHAPTER SEVEN: **the shopping, serving and storing**

The colors. The bottle designs. The bottle shapes.

What is happening?

Shopping for pink wines has become a lot more involved these days.

Back in the day, acquiring a bottle of rosé would be more of a grab-and-go endeavor.

You'd check the price, make sure the color was correct and – if the label was presentable enough – you'd be paid up, out the door and on the way to your destination.

It was a fairly no-brainer decision.

Not anymore!

My, my, how things have changed.

Those were also the days – closer to the year 2010 – when there were just a handful of options on the shelf.

With this rise in popularity over the last five to ten years, the amount of pink wine options is just bananas.

Now you are bound to view a sea of rosé wine options found in its very own section, and in some cases, in its very own isle.

It can be overwhelming.

There is one major theme when shopping for rosé, however, that remained constant: many customers continue to make purchase decisions based on the packaging.

When it comes to selecting a wine to purchase, order or serve, the "eyes" have it.

Rosé wine producers have always been very savvy in their presentation of their wines. Unlike red wines and many white wines on the shelf, rosé bottles are made of clear glass. That decision was made to show off the color in the rosé.

We know very well that consumers have specific interests regarding the color of the rosé, based on what's popular or based on their individual preferences.

Selling wine by enhancing the packaging has become even more prevalent within the pink wine category with all the emerging trends hitting the market.

New bottle shapes and packaging are slowly flooding the market as innovation is fueling the war for attention and market share.

Some bottles look like very traditional wine bottles, but they feature elaborate labels that speak to the "good life" or celebrate the seasonality surrounding rosé consumption.

There is a new wave of bottles shapes. Many of the new standout options are either square shaped or they resemble your Grandmother's rose perfume mister.

And then there are the packaging options that extend way beyond the glass bottle: plastic bottles, cans, boxes, wine pouches and – in some cases – rosé kegs. Yes, even kegs.

It's a very exciting thing to see. However, it could be both a blessing and a curse for consumers.

The clever packaging can distract the customer. It can be so convincing in its sales strategy that it takes the focus off two very important things: the sense of place and the quality of the wine.

For many rosé consumers, where the rosé comes from is inconsequential. And that's understandable. The color and style of rosé have been more important to consumers in many cases.

But what about the quality? What about the taste?

Is a pretty package more important than the juice in the bottle?

These are new considerations consumers must contend with as they approach shopping for rosé wines these days.

However, just like any decision related to wine, it's a personal one. It ultimately goes back to personal preferences, personal palates and deciding what is best for the situation.

In this chapter, we'll illuminate some of the common questions many of my wine consumers and students have had over the years in relation to shopping for, serving and storing their rosé wines.

Then we'll delve into some nuanced elements to help consumers feel more empowered when it comes to their pink wine purchase decisions.

: the shopping — the pricing

Regardless of the wine category you are shopping for, price is always an important factor.

Pink wines are no exception.

Rosé wine options have been massively embraced over the last 10 years partly because of price. Consumers love that most pink wines on the market are both high-quality and affordable.

You could spend anywhere between $10 to $20 on a good rosé and be very happy. Fortunately, that is still the case – for most rosé options.

However, prices are changing a bit. Part of it is simply that the cost of business goes up little by little from year to year and that affects the market-rate price.

As you become older, you'll see the slight increases and soon turn into your grandparents reminiscing about how little rosé used to cost "back in the day."

Then you add supply and demand to the equation and the price starts to increase. Rosé is so popular, especially the ones from Provence, the supply is effectively meeting the

> rosés can now cost up to $200 per bottle

demand today. But as rosé becomes more popular, and if the region remains the go-to region for pink wine, customers will start to see incremental increases in the coming years as the region works to keep up with the growing demand.

One element many of us – wine professionals and consumers – didn't see coming is the entrance of "luxury" rosé wine options.

Outside of the standard $10 to $20 range, we've seen some rosé wines inch closer to $25 to $30. And, of course, there are some of the classic Provence rosé producers that have historically sold their rosé wines for around $50 per bottle.

These days, there are pink wines from Provence, Languedoc-Roussillon, Spain and the United States, selling between $35 to $200 per bottle. That's not a typo: $200 per bottle.

These new price points, along with the growing popularity of pink wine, could inspire other producers to think differently, especially if a strong market surfaces for these higher priced options.

Today the sweet spot for pricing is $10 to $25 per bottle for a quality rosé. Yet again, like anything with wine, it's a personal choice based on your preferences, palates, the situation – and in this case – your budget.

: the shopping — the colors

This is the time when we re-address that Pink Elephant in the room. I'm referring to the info brought up in CHAPTER TWO: **the styles and structures**.

It's the color of pink wine.

If repetition is the effective teaching tool that I think it is, you can fill in these blanks from memory the certain style that has become super mainstream:

_____,_____,_____,_____,_____.

That style of wine – while amazingly delicious and currently chilling in my glass while I'm typing this out – has dominated the pink wine category.

This style has done wonders for the rosé category. It has entered the hearts, minds and consciousness of consumers around the world – adding some much-needed legitimacy to the pink wine world.

As a pink wine fan, I am forever grateful for this style and this winemaking region. I will be buying and consuming and celebrating the good life as much as possible.

Let's drink to many more successful years to come!

The only caveat is that with the lion share of attention on that "signature style," it can unintentionally have a cannibalizing effect on other styles – particularly the styles that are deeper and darker in color.

There is a common perception that deeper, darker rosés are going to be "sweet" or "sweeter" than the pale, light, dry, crisp styles. As a result, consumers might see a Petite Sirah rosé from California, a Garnacha rosado from Spain, or a Cerasuolo d'Abruzzo from Italy, and pass it up because of its color.

I've also addressed this briefly in the second chapter, but it is especially fitting here.

The color does not affect the sugar content of the wine.

Winemakers can regulate how light or dark they want the wine. And in a separate action, they can determine how dry or sweet they want the wine.

The two processes are not linked together. Therefore, you can have a deep, dark Petite Sirah from California and it will be very dry – meaning little to no residual sugar. Or you can have a light pink wine that is semi-sweet.

What the deeper, darker color can provide the wine, however, is more weight and complexity. The wine soaks up more characteristics from the skins, particularly the color, but also the tannins, flavors and phenols from the skin contact.

That can open your rosé consumption up to a richer, sometimes smoother mouthfeel. Then, in terms of food and wine pairings, these deeper rosé wines that pair better with more heartier dishes like the kind you will find grilled in the summer or served at winter holiday celebrations.

Therefore, please do not judge a rosé by its color. You could really be missing out on an extraordinary experience with a lovely rosé.

: the shopping — the vintage

The vintage of a wine can be very perplexing for shoppers.

Essentially, the vintage of a wine is the year that the grapes were turned into wine.

Grapes have a growing cycle every year, in both the Northern and Southern Hemispheres. The year the grapes are picked and turned into wine is the vintage year listed on the bottle.

If grapes were picked in 2011, then the wine is a 2011 vintage pink wine. If grapes were picked in 1979 and turned into Champagne, then that is a 1979 vintage rosé Champagne.

The confusion oftentimes sets in when *one* word has *two* different meanings that are applied to the wine world. In this case, it is the word "vintage." Sometimes wine is referred to as a "vintage" wine. In that context, that means it is an older wine.

Many consumers have a strong preoccupation with the vintage of wine when shopping.

It is my belief that it goes back to prestige and a common belief that "wine is better with age."

While that can be true of some wines, the "better with age" notion does not apply to all wines – especially with most rosé wine.

Some wines will expire sooner than others – especially with most rosé wine.

These are some wines that are meant to be consumed quite young – one year to about three years of the wine's vintage. The potential of these wines will peak early, and the wine starts to decline in character and structure inside the bottle. If held for too long before opening and consuming, the rosé can smell and taste like vinegar once its finally opened.

: the shopping — the older vintages

Not to confuse the issue, but there are some still (non-sparkling) rosé wines that are meant to age and can be quite beautiful and interesting.

These styles are representative of the classic Provence styles coming from the Bandol region, some of the deeper, dark-pink styles with more body, and some of the higher priced options.

Winemakers from around the world are now looking into producing some age-worthy rosé wines to potentially expand the pink wine market and offer something that will stand up as a "collectable" rosé. Those are wines we might see hit the market within the next five to ten years.

However, currently, most aged rosé wines you are more likely to find on the market are in the form of sparkling rosé wines made in the Champagne method.

These include Champagnes, Cavas and other styles around the world have some aging already built in because of the process. The amounts of acid and alcohol in these pink sparkling wines make them suitable to rest and cellar for decades.

The important thing to note is that these wines have aging potential. The key word being "potential." Sometimes wines do not live up to their potential for a variety of reasons: production methods, wine damage or taint of some kind.

But many times, if a wine doesn't live up to its potential, it could be due to human error.

We will go over that towards the end in the storage section of this chapter.

: the shopping — the bottle closures

I've experienced this dilemma first-hand.

Over the years, I have worked on many wine store's sales floors.

I listen to the customer's request. Then I skillfully pick out the ideal bottle for them – if I do say so myself – only to be confronted with the phrase: "Oh, I don't like wines with a screw top."

The apprehension is real.

There can be a lot of anxiety in terms of what type of closure is on the wine bottle.

It can be an immediate deal breaker for some consumers.

This has become a major issue in the pink wine category as many producers don't choose to utilize the classic closures.

However, it's a situation that can be worked through. It just takes some perspective, which link back to some of the initial questions I posed at the beginning of the chapter.

Is the goal of the purchase to get a nice-looking bottle or is the goal to get a great tasting wine?

Because unfortunately, sometimes getting a great bottle with the ideal closer does not always equate to enjoyable juice in the container.

The question is now, what are the differences in closures?

In terms of closures, the overarching goal is to seal the wine away from oxygen and other elements like dust, dirt, debris.

But to answer that question more thoroughly, we'll need to delve deeper into the major types of bottle closures and determine how these styles might factor into your decision-making process.

: the cork

Cork is familiar and comforting to wine lovers. There is a certain elegance, a certain cachet associated with opening a bottle of wine with a cork stopper. It is also the "Pomp and Circumstance" when it comes to the wine bottle presentation at a lovely restaurant or during a special occasion or just in general.

Cork is a natural material shaved from the bark of two different types of oak trees that grow in regions of the Northwest part of Africa and in Southwest Europe. Besides it being a mainstay in the wine world, the properties of cork are beneficial to the long-term storing and aging of wine. Since cork is porous – full of tiny spaces – it allows for micro-oxygenation or the flow of oxygen into the wine.

However, with cork being a natural material, there are some downsides that come with using cork to seal off wine bottles. The first major issue is the risk of TCA taint or "cork taint." This essentially occurs when the TCA chemical compound leaches unfavorable smells and flavors into the wine that might be associated with wet newspaper, damp cloth or a mildew in basements.

Then there comes the fragility of cork when improperly stored or from extended aging. Cork can easily dry out if the bottle is stored improperly over a long period of time. Once that happens, the cork can fall apart when being removed by a wine key / corkscrew. Then you need clever ways of getting the cork out, either using a two-prong cork puller or pushing the cork into the bottle.

While the latter is not harmful for the wine, it does make fishing those pieces out of the wine or glass annoying.

Lastly, cork is shaved from trees. If overdone, it can have negative environmental effects and result in instituting necessary conservation and / or reforestation efforts.

Cork is an optional choice for winemakers. Some love it and some choose to go a different route. However, when it comes to the pink wines that are meant to age a while, cork will probably always have a role in helping those wines progress over time.

That's the real cork stopper. Next up we have the synthetic corks.

These would be the middle ground between traditional corks and screw caps. It's an alternative that offers up some of that ceremonial pleasure while guarding against the potential contamination of the wine by TCA.

: the screw cap

Seeing a screw cap does not visually always connect to what some consumers might consider a "quality wine."

For them, it screams "cheap" or "unsophisticated" or even "gauche."

Before we judge these closures, let's get to understand them better.

Primarily called Stelvin tops, the goal of these screw caps is to make opening easier, protect against contamination, preserve aromas and freshness, and ensure a quality product is delivered to consumers.

These metal screw caps feature a perforated top and a long outside skirt. This skirt resembles the foil on the bottle of a cork stopper.

However, these types of closures were not very well received when the wine world, a few decades back, was undergoing a renaissance of sorts globally. From the late 1970s onward, the focus was on quality, prestige and luxury.

It was a departure from the casual consumption of wine in the 1960s and early 1970s when many wines were sold as inexpensive bulk wines.

After being reintroduced in the late 1980s and early 1990s, the concept of screw caps on wine started to stick a bit more around the world. New World markets like Australia and New Zealand were the early adapters of using screw caps as the standard closure for most of their wines.

Usage of screw caps nearly doubled and tripled in some cases in those areas and the pink wine category had a lot to do with that.

: the glass stopper

This is sort of the cool, mysterious new kid on the block.

It's stylish. It's sophisticated. It's unique. It seems to have some type of elevated status and distinct function.

These newer glass stoppers stand out to both winemakers and consumers alike. For winemakers, the stoppers prevent cork damage to the wine. And for customers, it looks like a more visually appealing alternative to screw caps.

Rosé winemakers are starting to incorporate these stoppers into their pink wine offerings to add a little extra layer of panache to the bottle.

Around the time rosé started to first experience a resurgence of interest, the stoppers were being produced in the early 2000s by a German company called Vino-Lok.

The bottle is typically sealed with a plastic cover over the glass stopper that can be removed with the knife on a wine key. Then there is a seal between the stopper and the bottle that is formed by a neutral polymer disk. The disk is resistant to both acid and alcohol. There is also technology built in that allows the stopper to allow oxygen in to let the wine breathe in the bottle.

Consumers have also come to enjoy these stoppers because it forms a tight closure. That allows you to preserve any left-over wine more effectively and slightly longer – like a screw cap – as it regulates how much air can get into the wine after being opened.

: the shopping — bottle shapes and sizes

Bottle shapes are one of the most festive aspects of the pink wine category.

But surprisingly enough, it is not a new concept.

Creating distinctive bottle shapes for rosé wine started in the early 1900s in Provence. René Ott of Domaine Ott started creating bottles molded after the shape of the old amphora clay wine vessels. That shape became their signature for the brand's prestige wines.

What is new, however, is the vast amount of different shapes hitting the market as rosé producers fight for the consumer dollar. Wine producers are also focusing on more larger format options, to coincide with the "party" lifestyle associated with rosé wine.

As mentioned previously, the addition of the new shapes can either be a blessing or a curse for the pink wine category.

The marketing goal for new brands is to cut through the clutter and sell the wine. That's a natural part of business.

Unfortunately, that can sometimes – from a professional perspective – bump up against the pink wine category's efforts to garner respect and be taken more seriously in the industry.

On the shelf, the winemaker and the wine region can become quite insignificant to customers thanks to the clever graphic design and distinctive bottle shape.

Before we focus on the shapes, let's shift gears a little bit and focus on size.

In terms of bottle sizes, the most common wine bottle is the 750ML size. However, wine bottles range from the single-serve size to very large formats to suit certain occasions.

The larger bottles of wine – ranging from the 1.5-liter, Magnum bottles (two bottles in one) to the "soirée-size" 3-liter bottles (four bottles in one) – are great for special occasions and parties.

Those sizes can equate to more fun and the ability to serve a larger number of people. This is especially true when you combine the larger size format with a quirky new bottle shape.

These new shapes are quite remarkable to behold. That goes for both the new shapes and the artful bottle designs on the traditional bottle types.

Here are some of the pink wine bottle shapes currently found on the market:

Square bottle – The square bottle has come along recently as a visual way to stand out among the various traditional bottles of wine, particularly in the pink wine space. Fairly reminiscent of a narrow perfume bottle – which Provence makes a lot of from the lavender fields there – this format comes in the standard 750ml size as well as larger formats.

Squat / Flask – This style has been associated with wines made in Portugal around World War II, most commonly associated with the Mateus brand. This bottle is shorter and resembles an army flask because the bottle is flat in nature. The design was based on a water flask or canteen that Portuguese soldiers used during the second world war. Some producers have implemented characteristics from this time into some of the perfume-esque bottles on the market.

Rosé à la parfume bottle – These wine bottles look like something from a high-end perfume counter. These bottles can be shorter in stature and wider in diameter. They can be made with etchings on taller bottles or can be made of sculpted glass. And they can have perfume-like decorated glass stoppers. The bottles are so visually appealing, many consumers hold on to them and repurpose them once the wine is gone.

Flûte à corset – In some circumstances, it looks like the bottle design embodies the shape of a person. Legend has it that the shape was modeled after the American actress, singer and sex symbol Mae West. Nicknamed as "aubergine," the bottle can also sometimes resemble an eggplant or a flower vase.

Alsace flûte — These bottles are tall, thin and represent wines that come from the Alsace region of France and from Germany. This bottle shape is also known as the Hock. Producers from Austria, Germany, Alsace and New York, tend to opt for this style. Some rosé producers use the general structure of this bottle and made modifications to the bottom for additional flair.

Champagne — All wines with bubbles are contained in a special sparkling wine bottle. These bottles hold Champagne, Cava, Prosecco, Sekt and other sparkling wines from around the world. This style of bottle is thicker and heavier than still, non-sparkling wine bottles. That is because it needs to successfully contain the high-pressure contents of the sparkling juice.

Bordeaux — The shape of these Bordeaux bottles is slender with noticeable shoulders near the neck of the bottle. They were used to contain wines made from traditional red Bordeaux blends featuring Cabernet Sauvignon and Merlot as well as the rosé Bordeaux blends. But many wine producing countries from around the world also use this shape. The curve on this bottle near the neck serve to trap sediment in the shoulder of the bottle of older red wines.

Burgundy — The Burgundy bottle is a little fuller than the Alsace flutes and has a slightly wider base than the Bordeaux bottles. This bottle shape was created sometime in the 19th century especially for Pinot Noir and Chardonnay wines. But many wine regions in France, Spain and the U.S. use them for a variety of rosé wine styles.

: the shopping — alternative packaging

Across the board, rosé drinkers tend to lean toward being fairly openminded and forward-thinking wine consumers.

I wouldn't image many of these consumers having a major issue with change and innovation.

But then again. You never know.

Some people don't do well with change, no matter how progressive they believe themselves to be.

Regardless of how you might feel about change, it is manifesting itself in the shape of alternative packaging. Many of these styles are already here and not going away any time soon.

When referring to alternative package, that means boxes, cans, plastic bottles, wine kegs and new wine pouches.

As our lives and daily behavior's change – how we entertain, socialize and travel – the wine world is adapting to those shifts by bringing new and interesting ways to engage and interact with wine.

The pink wine category has been on the front lines of those changes.

Let's take a quick look at the emerging trends, both at what's currently on the market and what's on the horizon.

Box Wines / Bag-in-Box (BIB) Wines – Box wines have provided large format wines, typically in the 3-liter to 5-liter sizes, for decades now. After years of being associated with "bulk" and "inexpensive" wines, select modern-day winemakers have taken a new liking to the format and use it as an alternative packaging to supplement many of their bottled wine offerings.

Essentially a Box Wine – or known as Bag-in-Box (BIB) wine – is wine placed in what's called a Polyethylene "bladder" and contained and dispensed from a corrugated, cardboard box.

Some boxes are even made of heavy pressed wood.

Thanks goes to the clever country of Australia for this addition to the wine world. The initial invention was in 1965. But with a few tweaks and a couple years later came the "pièce de résistance:" the plastic, air-tight spout attached to the bladder. This helps keeps oxygen away from the wine, which prolongs the freshness of the wine for up to three weeks.

Box wines are ideal for a variety of consumers. It's suited for those who want fresh wine daily, but only drink one glass per day. And it's ideal for those on a budget who want to enjoy wine regularly without breaking the bank.

They were once used to sell inexpensive bulk wines. That is still a big part of the business. However, the quality of wine found in many box-wine brands has improved over previous years.

Part of its popularity is being pushed forward by Millennials who enjoy more casual approaches to wine. Its lower price points don't hurt either. Others enjoy the fact that Box wines have a lower carbon footprint compared to bottles because they are lighter and easier to transport, helping to reduce carbon-dioxide emissions.

Wine in Cans – The canned wine segment has been steadily growing in popularity resulting in a $70 million business annually with growth predictions through 2025.

With the rapid growth of rosé globally and the popularity of cans, the two combined are a love match for the market.

Like box wines, select modern-day winemakers have sought out cans as an alternative package to their bottled wine options. Some companies offer their wine in bottles, boxes and cans. And some companies exclusively offer wine in cans.

Most can wine options come in the 375ML size, which is about 2 1/2 glasses of wine. Other smaller options come in between 250ML and 187ML sizes.

Again, these are not wines for cellaring. These wines are meant to be consumed young and fresh in more casual settings. Some of the traits that attract consumers to can wines is that there is no corkscrew or glassware needed. And the cans are lightweight, easy to transport and travel with, and they dispose of easily when its empty.

Wine in Pouches – This is a product that is currently being released to select markets with the health driven, eco-conscious consumer in mind.

This new packaging takes the pouch concept out of the box and gives it a makeover to look and feel more presentable in public.

Creating ripple effects in the United Kingdom and in the U.S., the new wine pouches focus on organic and biodynamic farming, sustainability and vegan wine production.

The bags come in 1.5-liter sizes, which is the equivalent of two bottles of wine. Like a bag-in-box – just without the box – the pouches have a vacuum seal and help reduce carbon emissions due to its packaging.

: the serving — serving temperature

If shopping for a rosé typically consisted of grab-and-go endeavor, serving pink wine would probably be as simple as these three steps: chill, pour and sip.

It would easy and straight-forward, right?

Yes, you can take that approach. But there are some helpful guidelines to follow to help maximize the enjoyment.

First things first. When serving wine, all wine should be served chilled.

That goes for red, white, rosé and orange wine.

> all wine should be
> served chilled

However, they should be chilled in varying degrees according to the style.

Still rosé wines should be *chilled* while sparkling rosé options, on the other hand, should be served *cold*.

Wine was meant to be served at cellar temperature. This temperature helps to properly show off the wine's structures and elements. I imagine that somewhere down the road as we progressed as a more modern society, cellar temperature got turned into room temperature in relation to serving wine.

Cellar temperature is a more constant temperature with very little variation. Those temperatures are between 50- and 65-degrees Fahrenheit, with an ideal average of about 55 degrees.

As a result, ideal serving temperatures are:

• Sparkling rosé wines — 40 to 45 degrees (cold, but not freezing)

- Light-bodied rosé wines — 50-55 degrees

- Medium-bodied rosé wines — 55-60 degrees

- Full-bodied rosé wines — 60-65 degrees

The key word here is "ideal." It is okay to drink your pink wines outside of cellar temperatures. But for maximum enjoyment, cellar temperature is best.

Rosé wine, no matter the body type, is not enjoyable at room temperature – especially sparkling rosé wine.

That is not fun for anyone. Trust me.

: the serving – rosé à la piscine

When in Provence, do as the Provençal people do!

That means you put ice in your rosé from time to time.

I know. I know. I know.

I'm sure I have some wine purists in here that can roll with the punches on a lot of these rosé practices.

But there are some people who will just draw the line. And it might be here.

Please just humor me for a few moments.

It is a long-standing practice to make the rosé as cold as possible in Provence to help combat the intense heat of the glorious Sun.

This is an actual custom of drinking pink wine with ice called rosé à la piscine. This is how wine is enjoyed by the swimming pool (piscine is pool in French), by the beach or just on an extraordinarily hot day in the South of France.

There can be some flavor issues with this, however. On a really hot day, the ice will melt quickly, leaving you by the pool with a severely watered-down glass of wine.

To offset that, some people add a little liqueur or ruby red grapefruit juice for additional flavor. That ensures that the flavor will last once the ice melts.

So, in a way, it becomes like a rosé cocktail.

For those who might be cringing at the thought of either adding ice or some form of spirit to your pink wine, I have a suggestion on how you can taste your rosé and drink it cold too.

However, it will take some forethought and planning on your end.

Keep a bag of frozen grapes in your freezer. When your rosé starts to get too warm in the summer sun, add some of your frozen grapes to the rosé and you'll lower the temperature and not lose any flavor.

: the serving — glassware

Glassware has a charming way of enhancing the wine experience – from the shapes to the stem heights to the brilliant sheen on a freshly polished bulb.

Glassware is important to the serving experience. That's without a doubt. There are glassmakers that make wine glasses to suit specific types of wines, from sparkling to Pinot Noir to Cabernet Sauvignon to Syrah.

These glasses are lovely because the bulbs are crafted and shaped to make the wine touch your palate a certain way in order to best show off the grape varietal.

But drinking a Bordeaux out of a Burgundy glass is not necessarily a deal-breaker. In fact, there are some regions around the world where people drink wine out of tumblers, and they are as happy as can be.

In the wine world, professionals opt to use what we call "A.P." (all-purpose) glasses. An all-purpose wine glass tends to resemble a Bordeaux-style glass. It has a tulip-shaped bulb that can hold 8 ounces of wine or more. We pour just about everything from these glasses including sparkling, red, white, rosé and orange wines.

Ideally you want the glass to be thin and be free of a bump or ridge around the rim of the glass. That sounds very particular, but you just want a clear path for the wine to enter your mouth. And, most importantly, you want to make sure the mouth of the bulb tapers inward. The mouth should be narrower than the center part of the bulb. This allows in the proper amount of air to adequately aerate the wine.

Glasses with stems are ideal for semi-formal to formal occasions. Typically, it is best to hold wineglasses by the stem. That helps keep the wine away from your body heat, which can warm up the wine too much. It also keeps the bulb free of fingerprints as oil and food can accumulate on the glass.

While stemless glasses are lovely, your fingers repeatedly touch the bulb and can leave tons of marks. These glasses are better suited for more casual situations, oftentimes perfect for rosé. You would just have to be cautious of your body heat warming up the pink wine.

There are lots of great glass options on the market, from the inexpensive to the wildly pricey. The best approach is to select glass options within your budget and personal style parameters.

But please do me a favor!

Bypass the plastic cocktail and soda cups for parties and picnics and such. There are lots of great seamless, plastic wine glass options for those times when proper wine glasses – or glass in general – are not viable options.

: the storing

In a grab-and-go pink wine world, there is not a lot of wine storage going on.

Most wine purchases are consumed within the first few hours of purchase and rosé might be even sooner than that. Once there is a nice chill on the bottle, it's pretty much a pour and sip proposition.

However, just like in the overall wine world, there are exceptions to every rule and for every situation.

It is true that most of the rosé wines on the market will be consumed right away.

But there are sometimes when you want to stock up – maybe for a special occasion, maybe for a season or maybe just to have around to enjoy at any time of the year.

Wine, regardless of the price, it is an investment and property you want to protect. You don't want to secure a case or two of rosé for a party only to open it a few weeks later to find that it tastes like vinegar because you stored it incorrectly.

Therefore, even if long-term storage, isn't on your radar with rosé. You should, at least, know the proper ways to store the pink wine so it is enjoyable when you get around to opening it.

Here are tips for successfully keeping your pink wines safe, healthy and secure.

: the storage — short-term

Cellaring wine for the short-term could mean anywhere from a few months to up to a few years. You might not want to invest too much money into storing these wines, but you want to protect them.

Here are some dos and don'ts to help you manage the process!

The Dos
• Do find a cool, dark place to store your wines: basement, closet, lower cabinet, storage bin under your bed
• Do store it in a low-lying place
• Do store the wine on its side
• Do invest in a small wine refrigerator
• Do secure wine storage companies for multiple bottles you can't manage on your own

The Don'ts
- Don't store on top of the refrigerator
- Don't expose the wine to sunlight
- Don't hang or store wine on high shelves or upper cabinets as rising heat can damage the wine
- Don't store the wine in an enclosed kitchen — this room is a constant source of heat fluctuations
- Don't forget that not all wine is meant to be aged

: the storage — the long-term

Long-term storage of your pink wines can be a great way to take special care of the more prestigious rosé wines you might acquire from traveling, as a gift or as part of a growing collection.

There are a variety of pink wines, still and sparkling, currently on the market that can benefit from the aging process. There also might be pink wine options that are produced to have up to a 10-year aging window hitting stores shelves in the future.

This collection of yours will be with you for maybe five, 10 or even 20-plus years for some sparkling wines.

This is a lot of responsibility. These bottles are your investment and you want to protect them from potentially harmful influences.

You can seek out help to professionally store your wine over time or take on the responsibility yourself.

For long-term storage, you want to create a space that closely resembles the traits of an underground wine cellar where these wines can rest.

If you have instructions to drink a wine between 2025 and 2030, you want to do your best to make sure it receives all the care and consideration it needs to mature properly. At the end of the cellaring time, you are hoping that your patience will have paid off and that the wine matured into a complex, dynamic wine.

A little organization goes a long way in managing a wine cellar. It can save you time, energy and money. And it can help prepare you for worst-case scenarios.

A classic wine cellar environment has been proven to be the most effective and ideal way of storing wine for the long haul. The cellar is consistent. The cellar is controlled. The cellar is still.

To mimic those underground cellar conditions in an above-ground location, the following strategies are vital to the process.

SECURE BOTTLES — Plan on the proper shelving or storage bins in which to place your wine. They should be sturdy and prevent the wines from rolling around. Wines should be laid on their sides with the labels facing up. The liquid should be in direct contact with the cork. This helps to keep the cork from drying out.

SMELLS — While you want to keep your cellar clean, you also want to keep it free of strong orders. That could be from bacteria, pests or even strong cleaning supplies. It is very easy for wine to pick up those aromas if exposed to them on a frequent basis.

INVENTORY — Depending on the size of your storing collection, the inventories should be labeled, numbered and catalogued. An inventory system will help you easily find bottles stored in the cellar. With the labels facing up, you can find and view the wines without causing disruption to other bottles. An inventory list is also perfect for insurance purposes. It comes in handy for those unexpected situations like theft, accidents or massive damage to your cellar.

DON'T BE AFRAID OF THE DARK — Committing to cellaring and storing wine until it matures is not for the faint of heart. And it's not for those who fear the dark. With wine already being a sensitive, living and breathing object, it cannot withstand too much light – particularly sunlight. Be sure to keep your wine away from windows or any constant, powerful sources of light.

CONSTANT TEMPERATURE — With an average temperature of 55 degrees, a cellar is a lot like springtime in the Midwest. It can be a little chilly. Be sure to bundle up with a cozy sweater. The wine, however, will be quite comfortable. This temperature allows the wine to age at a slow and steady pace. If the space is too hot, that starts to accelerate the aging of the wine. Conditions that are too cold could cause the wines to frost or freeze. That could potentially push the cork out some, allowing air to get into the bottle.

HIGH HUMIDITY — This is not like being in the tropics or the Gulf of Mexico. However, a certain amount of humidity – around the 60 to 80 percent mark – is great for the cork. It helps to keep the cork intact, along with resting the bottles horizontally for constant contact with the wine. Humidity levels below 50 percent can lead to the cork drying out, causing spills, oxidation and extreme mold.

BREATHING ROOM — While the cellar is dark and cool in temperature, it doesn't mean the room's air has to be stuffy or stale. Proper ventilation is how a wine cellar maintains a consistent temperature. Investing in a cooling unit and exhaust system is necessary for the health of the bottles. It keeps the cool air in and pushes the warm air out.

AVOID DISRUPTIONS — The cellar should be a still, quiet place. It is not the place for a flurry of activity or tomfoolery. There is no need to constantly move or handle the bottles. Too many vibrations and disturbances can really disrupt the wine's rest. Let sleeping bottles lie. And enjoy the fruitful reward of your patience in the years to come.

: the gratitude

I am feeling grateful AF!

Do not get me wrong. This has been one hell of a year – and, we all know, that is not anything great to write home about.

It has taken many deep breaths, a lot of burning sage, a lot of thinking and a lot of wine to get me to this point.

These challenging, dark times that I find myself facing were enough to make me want to crawl under the covers and not come out until all was right in the world again.

In those moments, I had to stay strong. I had to stay positive. I had to stay grateful.

Moving forward through these recent dark times, step by step, is what kept this book alive. It is what helped keep my spirit alive. And it is what helped me keep my hope alive.

Despite what 2020 has presented, I am thankful for this life. I am thankful for these breaths that I am blessed enough to take. And I am thankful for this fight within me to keep moving forward.

For all those varied reasons – and many more – I will state it again: I am GRATEFUL AF!

: the acknowledgments

This type of long form writing project can get very quiet and very lonely at times.

It is a highly solitary act.

For the most part, it is just you and your computer. You spend more time connecting with the keys on the keyboard than you do with actual people in most cases.

That is because that type of writing takes a lot of patience. It takes peace. It requires going deep into research and then deep into your own head. It requires deep concentration.

But people are also crucial to the process. People fill in the gaps; the gaps between the keystrokes, the pregnant pauses, the frustrated sighs and the exhilaration of promising prose breakthroughs.

They fill in those gaps with joy, comfort, check-ins, human connection and support.

And despite being engulfed in your literary world for however long, they are there, eagerly waiting for you to share the finished piece with them and celebrate your contribution to the world.

I want to thank all the people who have played a role on my journey of releasing this new book.

First and foremost, I want to thank my immediate family: Mom, Simba and Storm. You three have been my life support as this project hit several bumps in the road. Thank you for keeping me and this book afloat.

Thank you to everyone who supported "The Less Is More Approach to Wine." All the love that was shown in terms of purchases, reviews, feedback and spreading the word really gave me the encouragement to jump right into this new book. Thank you to Ms. Blanche for suggesting that I add photos to the book. It made quite the difference.

That initial support paved the way for an exciting and heart-warming promotional book tour. Big thanks go out to Daneen and Pascale of Harlem Wine Gallery; Hugues, Eliot, Sharon and Roman at Roma Wine & Liquor on the Upper West Side; Gary at Taste Wine Co. in the East Village; Daniel at Boswell Books in Milwaukee, Wisconsin and my lovely book signing moderator and fellow author Vivian King; Tom and team at EBANMAN Inc./Lifestyle Magazine, in Chicago and Atlanta; The Wine Avengers (Larissa, Sukari and Jermaine); Jeryl and Ty of Off The Rox in Baltimore; Mark and Katrina of the NiLu Gift Shop in Harlem; Cuisine Noir Magazine and V. Sheree Publishing; and Sally and Sandye of "Pop Pairings" TV.

Continued thanks go to some of my long-time supporters: Shane, Arturo, Juan Carlos, Fernando and Narissa at NYVintners; Laura, Greg, Isaiah, Ehron, Dorian, Andrew, Ryan, Amber, Kim. Jaime and Humberto at Corkbuzz; Jamie and the recommendation specialist team at Wine.com; Susan at Urban Uncorked; Chef Ryan of Fork & Saber; Lea of Let's Talk Wine; Charles of Hamilton Wine House; and Colin and Gabby at BTL; the entire team at the Sommelier Society of America; Sud du France / Maison de la Region Occitanie New York and all the teams and individuals who brought me into their tastings, events, celebrations and gatherings.

Thank you to you all my dear friends that have been so super supportive these last 12 months: Dr. Sherri, Jermaine, Paul G., Cynthia, Shea, Carrie, Lisa, Cassie, Theresa, Sohad, Bruno, Keith, Chris, Andre, Nicole, Kristina, Jessica, Amanda, Julie, Vince, Syndee, Derrick, Brenae, Lauren, Kara, Edwin, Lauren, Rachel, Demetrius, C.J., KT, Vonnie, Maxwell, Jannelle.

To my Black Wine Lovers family: Cha, Shakera, George, Joni, Lia, Julia, DLynn, Tahiirah, Derrick W., Kelly, Lia, Tuanni, and countless others across the country. I can't forget about my Black Food Folks including Clay, Colleen, Bryan, Keesha, Annette, etc.

A special thank you goes out to my very special Tish Around Town Chat 'n Sip Quarantine family starting with the lady herself Tish. We've had an amazing time hosting the sip and chat education sessions. It really helped get me through the pandemic. Then I was fortunate enough to have met so many others along the way, like Lorraine, Jenn, Stephanie, Terry, Mialeeka, Kanika, Kim, Kindralyn, Donae, Coviello and the slew of others who have joined throughout the spring. I'm glad Toussaint joined us for the journey.

I knew taking on another book so soon after completing my first one would be a challenge. No one would know all the adversity, pain, dark times and uncertainty we would face moving into a new year and a new decade. The love and support and encouragement of my nearest and dearest. You really helped get me through the Rona isolation and through the senseless violence against our Black brothers and sisters.

Thank you all for being there on the other end of the phone, on Facetime, in person, in my head, in my heart and in my life.

This book would not be possible without the support of many of you.

For that, I'm eternally grateful and wanted to be able to acknowledge you all properly.

Much love!

~ Charles Springfield

: the author

Charles Dion Springfield is a Certified Sommelier in New York City where he developed a tailor-made lifestyle brand called "The Life Stylings of Charles Springfield." The company focuses on his approach to wine, events and joie de vivre (joy of life). The three major divisions include: The Wine Stylings, The Editorial Stylings and The Event Stylings.

He specializes in matching the right wines with the right people and occasions, teaching wine classes, hosting wine events and promoting overall wine appreciation through education.

Prior to falling headfirst into the wine business, he was an award-winning journalist and public relations executive for nearly two decades. As a print journalist, Charles began his career as a general assignment reporter at the Pulitzer-prize winning "Times-Picayune" daily newspaper in New Orleans. He has written columns and covered everything from crime and health to entertainment and lifestyle feature stories at "The Clarion-Ledger."

In the public relations field, he worked primarily in the consumer marketing / lifestyle realm at three advertising agencies and one boutique public relations firm.

For nearly ten years now he has used his unique approach to marketing communications, his "life styling" experience and love of wine to provide guidance on appreciating, understanding and enjoying wine in ways people never imaged possible.

Charles holds a Bachelor and a Master of Science degree in Mass Communication, both obtained from Jackson State University in Jackson, Mississippi. He is also certified by the Sommelier Society of America which was founded in 1954 and based in New York City.

: the wine terms

To help maximize the information in this book, I thought it would be helpful for to provide some topics and terms that can either serve as a refresher or a foundation for the reader. Feel free to revisit it as a point of reference.

: wine – an alcoholic beverage made from any fermented fruit juice – primarily grapes – as well as other items like rice and honey

: vitis vinifera: the "wine grape" species of grapes with origins in the Mediterranean region

: vitis labrusca: the grape species associated with origins in North America

: grape varietal / varieties – the name or type of grape used to make a wine (i.e. Chardonnay, Pinot Noir, Cabernet Sauvignon, Chenin Blanc, Concord, Niagara)

: fermentation – the metabolic process involved in the production of making wine, beer, spirits; in this case, it is the process of converting grapes into wine

: fermentation process: yeast + sugar = alcohol (ethanol), heat and CO_2 (carbon dioxide)

: fermentation vessels – a container or various containers used to ferment wine: amphora clay pots, kvevri/qvevri pots, concrete eggs, neutral oak barrels, seasoned oak barrels, stainless steel tanks, plastic tanks

: viticulture – the agricultural process involving the farming of grapes also known as vine agriculture; a branch of the science of horticulture

: **viticulturalist** – the person responsible for managing the agricultural process involving the farming of grapes

: **oenology / enology** – the art, science and study of making wine

: **oenologist / enologist** – the person or persons responsible for the science of winemaking

: **winemaker** – a producer of wine

: **red wine** – wine made from red skin grapes (red, blue, purple skins) with juice to skin contact for long durations of time to allow the skins to leech a strong concentration of color into the juice

: **rosé wine** – the popular and commonly used French term to call pink wine made from red skin grapes (red, blue, purple skins) with a short duration of juice to skin contact; the skin leeches small amounts of color into the juice; these wines can also be made with a blend of red and white wine in some cases

: **blush wine** – a popular term coined in the 1970s that refers to pink wine or rosé wine that typically stems from California; can be sweet or semi-sweet with a moderate- to low-alcohol content of 10 percent or less

: **pink wine** – a modern, pop-culture term used that refers to all pink-colored or rosé-colored wine from around the world

: **rosado wine** – the Spanish term for pink wine made from red skin grapes (red, blue, purple skin) in Spain and Portugal with a short duration of juice to skin contact; the skin leeches small amounts of color into the juice; these wines can also be made with a blend of red and white wine in some cases

: **rosato wine** – the Italian term for pink wine made from red skin grapes (red, blue, purple skin) in Italy with a short duration of juice to skin contact; the skin leeches small amounts of color into the juice; these wines can also be made with a blend of red and white wine in some cases

: **vin gris** – the French term literally translates in English to "gray wine" as a middle ground between the originally references of "black" and "white" grapes; it describes a very specific style of rosé wine that has minimal juice to skin contact producing an extremely pale rosé

: **white wine** – wine made from white skin grapes (yellow, gold, green, gray-ish skins) with no juice to skin contact and therefore no color is derived from the grape skins

: **orange wine** – wine made from white skin grapes (yellow, gold, green, gray-ish skins) with juice to skin contact for a select time period to achieve a range of colors from amber to orange and copper to light ruby

: **still wine** – a wine of any color that does not have any significant level of bubbles caused by trapped CO_2 or carbon dioxide after fermentation; some still wines can have a very minute amount of residual carbon dioxide in the bottle

: **sparkling wine** – a wine of any color that has a substantial level of bubbles caused by trapped CO_2 or carbon dioxide after fermentation

: **dry wine** – a wine of any color that has little to no residual sugar left in the wine after the fermentation process; the polar-opposite of sweet wines

: **semi-sweet wine** – a wine of any color that has a moderate amount of residual sugar left in the wine after the fermentation process

: **sweet wine** – a wine of any color that has a substantial amount of residual sugar left in the wine after the fermentation process

: **organic farming** – farming without the use of chemical pesticides, herbicides, fungicides, or in other words, an all-natural farming practices

: **sustainable farming** – farming that takes into consideration supporting the environment for the long-term future through a variety of practices including reducing the carbon footprint, water conservation, energy conservation and reusable resources – which most times utilizes natural or organic farming practices

: **biodynamic farming** – a farming practice started in the 1920s by Austrian scientist Rudolf Steiner that promotes natural, homeopathic ways of caring for the larger ecosystem of the wine region; vineyard management involves using the lunar calendar as a planting and harvesting schedule for farming

: **alcohol** – one of the main structures of wine; alcohol / ethanol is a natural intoxicant that is produced by the natural fermentation of sugars in wine, beer and spirits

: **body** – the texture or weight of wine felt on the palate (roof of mouth and tongue), ranging from light, medium to full

: **aromas** – the smell, aka nose, of wine based on chemical formulas that give off scents of grass, fruit, florals, herbs, vegetal, chemicals and an array of other aromatic notes

: **acidity** – an important structure found in all wines that gives them freshness and personally ranging from sharp (high acid) or mellow (moderate to moderate-minus acid) in terms of mouthfeel; it is based on the grape and growing conditions that makes mouths water (salivate) and refreshes palates with each sip

: **minerality** – another important structure of wines based on the soil's mineral composition – rocks and metals – in specific areas where the vines are planted that show off a part of the region's land

: **tannins** – a structure found in wines that have skin to juice contact; a natural astringent, which has a tactile dehydrating feeling, but also serves as a natural preservative

: **sulfites** – a naturally occurring byproduct in wine – also known as sulfur dioxide – caused by the fermentation of grapes that helps prevent bacteria and mold growth and maintains its freshness by working as a natural preservative

: **hectolitre / hectoliter** – a hectoliter is a metric unit of capacity that is equal to one hundred litres / liters.

: **the wine world** – wine-making regions ideal for grape growing that typically fall in between the 30th to 50th parallels in both the Northern and Southern Hemispheres

: **terroir** – the overall environment in which the grape grow that contribute to the smell, taste and texture of wines and provide a strong "sense of place"

: **old world regions / wines** – winemaking regions that have been making wine for 2,000 to 4,000 years (France, Italy, Spain, Germany, Portugal)

: **new world regions / wines** – winemaking regions that have been making wine for 200-400 years (Australia, New Zealand, North America, South America, South Africa)

: **ancient wine regions** – wine regions associated with winemaking for 8,000 to 10,000 years (Georgia, Slovenia, Egypt, China, Turkey

Made in the USA
Columbia, SC
22 September 2020